HEARING

Him

THE SAVIOR'S VOICE
in the
BOOK OF MORMON

Praise For
Hearing Him

"Diony and Trent Heppler demonstrate through their personal experiences that selected scriptural passages within *The Book of Mormon* provide the seeds of faith to learn and act upon, as guided by the Spirit. As the Church prepares to read *The Book of Mormon* for the 2024 Come Follow Me course, this book can become an essential guide to enhance one's testimony of this sacred scripture. They show how daily immersion in, and pondering the lessons within *The Book of Mormon*, has the power to change one's life for the better."

David R. Hocking, Managing Editor of the
Annotated Edition of *The Book of Mormon,
Another Testament of Jesus Christ*

"Diony and Trent Heppler's book offers inspiring answers to life's challenges. It is thought-provoking and yet easy to read. It empowers us as we focus on our Heavenly Father's love and guidance. Readers will find real meaning to their journeys on earth as they open their hearts to the Savior's voice in *The Book of Mormon*."

Sean Kikkert, author of *Last Days: How You
Can Prepare for the Lord's Second Coming*

"Diony and Trent Heppler have written a warm and thoughtful book to help us better hear the Lord's voice. Their focus on doctrines found throughout *The Book of Mormon* brings the reader into the details of that sacred book of scripture. This book is a perfect companion to your Book of Mormon study."

Aaron Bujnowski, co-author of *Discovering
Your Temple Insights*

"Diony and Trent have delivered insightful and heartfelt messages for the modern Latter-day Saint as they combine scripture with personal experiences creating a way for the reader to understand how to personalize the Book of Mormon. I love the readability of their book's smaller sections broken into chunks of wisdom and the overall message that Heavenly Father has given us the scriptures as a guide and gift for leading our lives."

Michelle Porcelli, author of *You Will Be
Found: How Heavenly Father Knows You and
Answers Your Prayers Individually*

DIONY & TRENT HEPPLER

HEARING

THE SAVIOR'S VOICE
in the
BOOK OF MORMON

CFI
An imprint of Cedar Fort, Inc.
Springville, Utah

ISBN 13 Paperback: 978-1-4621-4519-5
ISBN Ebook: 978-1-4621-4520-1

Published by CFI, an imprint of Cedar Fort, Inc.
2373 W. 700 S., Suite 100, Springville, UT 84663
Distributed by Cedar Fort, Inc., www.cedarfort.com

Library of Congress Registration Number: 2023941146

Cover design by Shawnda Craig
Cover design © 2023 Cedar Fort, Inc.
Edited by Liz Kazandzhy
Typeset by Liz Kazandzhy

Printed in the United States of America

10 9 8 7 6 5 4 3 2 1

Printed on acid-free paper

Other Books by Diony Heppler

Torn Apart

Imperfectly Beautiful

A Sisterhood of Strength

Heaven's Just a Prayer Away

God is With Us: How We Hear Him

Other Books by Trent Heppler

The Power Within

God is With Us: How We Hear Him

CONTENTS

ACKNOWLEDGMENTS

WE OFFER OUR SINCERE AND SPECIAL THANKS TO AMBRI, AMY, Breanna, Brian, Carol, Charlotte, Christi, Emily, Kelly, Lily, Mike, Tara, Todd, and Tom for so willingly sharing your personal insights and thoughts in this book as you have heard the Savior's voice while reading the Book of Mormon. We hope that together we can inspire many, many others to seek out direction and answers of their own.

PREFACE

It was Memorial Day Weekend in 2022, and we had taken a trip to the Ozarks in Eureka Springs, Arkansas, about four hours from our home. Neither of us had visited there before, and we were looking forward to a long weekend of relaxing and sightseeing. We enjoyed the charm of the town's mountainside steep-winding streets and pathways, its Victorian architecture, and learning its history about the reputed healing waters of Basin Spring.

One afternoon, our sightseeing adventures took us to Branson, Missouri, about an hour northeast of Eureka Springs. We had purchased tickets for a live show, something Branson is famous for, but we had some time to spare before it started. In my enduring love to shop, and Trent's patient willingness to make me happy, we found an eclectic group of antique and craft stores located under one roof where we stopped in to browse. One of the stores was selling books. While thumbing through a stack of biblical daily devotions, inspiration and ideas for this book began to form.

We hadn't planned on beginning another book just a few short months after finishing our last one, *God is With Us: How We Hear Him*, but the prompting and feelings to move forward by continuing our focus on "hearing Him" grew. We love receiving direction from the Spirit, but sometimes when what He wants us to do isn't easy—or in this case requires a lot of time and effort—it can feel daunting and overwhelming. However, we know from many past secular and spiritual experiences we've had, individually and as husband and wife, that He always provides a way.

President Eyring put it this way: "You show your trust in Him when you listen with the intent to learn and repent and then you go and do whatever He asks. If you trust God enough to listen for His message . . . you will find it. And if you then go and do what He would have you do, your power to trust Him will grow."[1]

We've both read the Book of Mormon several times before but would definitely admit we still have a lot to learn from its sacred pages. This time as we read it—specifically focusing on ways to hear God for ourselves, and seeking what He needed us to learn, understand, and share in this book—the experience was profound and wonderfully different. Our desire to study continually with greater commitment has increased, because though this experience, the Book of Mormon became more personalized.

Our love for the Book of Mormon prophets has grown—their faith, their humanness, their struggles, their courage, their endurance despite trials of many kinds, their love and sorrow for their families and brethren who turned away from God, their boldness of speech in declaring truth, their firmness to follow Christ. We could go on and on. All of them taught and inspired us in different ways.

As we have studied, read, and written what we've felt from specific scriptures that stood out during the compilation of this manuscript, the Spirit has been with us daily in greater abundance. Our understanding of the messages in the Book of Mormon has been enlarged as we've seen the scriptures through "new eyes." Noticeably, we have sensed a greater peace and light enter our lives on a consistent basis. The effect this has had on us individually and collectively has been a greater desire to be kinder, more patient, more forgiving, and more readily able to see the good in ourselves and others. We hope this can be defined as "more Christlike."

This experience has been an amazing gift—something we want for all of you! As you read the insights gained by us and by others who contributed to this book, we hope it ignites in you a desire to also hear Him better while you read and study the Book of Mormon for yourself.

INTRODUCTION

PRESIDENT RUSSELL M. NELSON HAS COUNSELED THAT "AS WE SEEK to be disciples of Jesus Christ, our efforts to *hear Him* need to be ever more intentional. It takes conscious and consistent effort to fill our daily lives with His words, His teachings, His truths."[1]

One place we can go to hear Him is the scriptures. "Daily immersion in the word of God is crucial for spiritual survival, especially in these days of increasing upheaval."[2] We have been promised that when we "feast upon on the words of Christ . . . the words of Christ will tell [us] all things what [we] should do" (2 Nephi 32:3).

The Book of Mormon, another testament of Jesus Christ, is an accounting of the rise and fall of two ancient civilizations that lived in the Americas. Several ancient prophets recorded their history in its pages through the spirit of prophecy and revelation. It includes a "crowning event," which is "the personal ministry of the Lord Jesus Christ among the Nephites soon after his resurrection. It puts forth the doctrines of the gospel, outlines the plan of salvation, and tells men what they must do to gain peace in this life and eternal salvation in the life to come" (introduction to the Book of Mormon).

Prophets have declared that the Book of Mormon was written for *our* day. They have also stated that "its narrative is a chronicle of nations long since gone. But in its descriptions of the problems of today's society, it is as current as the morning newspaper and much more definitive, inspired, and inspiring concerning the solution of those problems. . . . No other written testament so clearly illustrates the fact that when men and nations walk in the fear of God and in obedience to his commandments, they prosper and grow."[3] However, when they refuse to follow Him and embrace sin without repentance through His atoning grace, they become lost.

"The Book of Mormon, one of the Lord's powerful keystones in this counteroffensive against latter-day ills, begins with a great parable of life, an extended allegory of hope versus fear, of light versus darkness, of salvation versus destruction. . . . Love. Healing. Help. Hope. The power of Christ to counter all troubles in all times—including the end of times. That is the safe harbor God wants for us. . . . That is the message with which the Book of Mormon begins, and that is the message with which it ends."[4]

As we prayerfully and regularly study the Book of Mormon, increasing our ability to hear Him, we can receive personally tailored direction, understanding, strength, and hope in our daily lives.

PART I

THE FIRST BOOK OF NEPHI
(ABOUT 600–570 BC)

"Something powerful happens when a child of God seeks to know more about Him and His Beloved Son. Nowhere are those truths taught more clearly and powerfully than in the Book of Mormon."

—President Russell M. Nelson[1]

1

HEAVENLY PARENTS

"I, Nephi, having been born of goodly parents, therefore I was taught somewhat in all the learning of my father." (1 Nephi 1:1)

As I was attending sacrament meeting one week and feeling the Spirit while listening to the speakers, my mind reflected on how Trent and I should start this book. I recalled the very first scripture in the Book of Mormon, one I've read many times. In this moment, I felt a prompting to look at it differently, and the familiar words "born of goodly parents" (1 Nephi 1:1) expanded to a new focus in my mind—"born of heavenly parents."

I was hearing Him. And as I thought about my heavenly parents, my heart was filled with overwhelming love—*from* them and *for* them.

Just like Nephi, the son of Lehi and Sariah, who begins the record of his people in the Book of Mormon, each of us born into this world received mortal bodies created by earthly parents. Despite the varied circumstances of our physical births, we can feel and understand that we are known, loved, and cherished by heavenly parents whose images we were created in.

Knowing we are literal children of God, "children of the most High" (Psalms 82:6), can bring us peace, comfort, and direction. Each of us, individually, is part of an eternal plan. The assurance of knowing who we are can give us increased understanding and self-worth.

As we learn, grow, and are tested by the trials of life while on this earth, we can progress until we are perfect, developing the divine nature we have inherited from our heavenly parents. Part of that progression is finding strength in the healing balm of Jesus Christ's Atonement when we falter and make mistakes while learning to face challenges and heartaches with fearless faith.

Prophets have counseled, "You need, more and more, to feel the perfect love which our Father in Heaven has for you and to sense the value he places on you as an individual. Ponder upon these great truths, especially in those moments when . . . you might otherwise wonder and be perplexed."[1]

We can know this for ourselves, for "the Spirit itself beareth witness with our spirit, that we are the children of God" (Romans 8:16).

Satan wants us to doubt our divine nature, and he takes every opportunity he can to throw up roadblocks to make us question it. This happened to a young woman involved in a serious car accident. Though her physical trauma was severe from the accident she caused, the emotional pain she felt about the other driver who lost their life was much greater. Because of her self-blame, she questioned how God could love her.

With time her physical suffering diminished, but her emotional and spiritual anguish continued. For more than a year, she pushed the internal pain deeper inside, creating numbing distance from her Heavenly Father. Finally, an inspired counselor encouraged her to write down and say several times each day, "I am a child of God."

"Writing the words was easy," the young woman recalls, "but I couldn't speak them. . . . That made it real, and I didn't really believe God wanted me as His child. I would curl up and cry."

Several months passed before she was able to complete the entire task daily. "I poured out my whole soul, pleading with God. . . . Then I began to believe the words."

This belief allowed the Savior to begin mending her wounded soul. The Book of Mormon brought her comfort and courage as she read about His Atonement.

"Christ felt my pains, my sorrow, my guilt," she concluded. "I felt God's pure love and had never experienced anything so powerful! Knowing I am a child of God is the most powerful knowledge I possess!"[2]

Growing to become perfect like our heavenly parents is "messy and hard," as Trent and I like to say, but it's supposed to be! We chose to come to earth to be proven and to see if we would follow God's commandments, but we didn't come to face it alone. We can be reassured that our elder Brother and Savior, Jesus Christ, is here to help us, for "this is [His] work and [His] glory—to bring to pass the immortality and eternal life of man" (Moses 1:39).

Self-Reflection:
Take a break right now to say out loud, "I am a child of God!" What does that truth mean to you?

2

FEELING THE SPIRIT

"And it came to pass that as he read, he was filled with the Spirit of the Lord." (1 Nephi 1:12)

IN THIS CHAPTER, NEPHI TELLS US ABOUT HIS FATHER, THE PROPHET Lehi, who "prayed unto the Lord . . . with all his heart, in behalf of his people" (1 Nephi 1:5), after which the Lord showed him many things in a vision. During the vision, he read from a book of prophecy and "was filled with the Spirit of the Lord" (1 Nephi 1:12). We too can hear Him through the Holy Ghost when we learn to recognize His presence through listening with our mind and our heart. We've been taught that the Holy Ghost can comfort, warn, testify, inspire, and guide us.

Jesus Christ promised His disciples during the Last Supper that after He departed out of the world to go "unto the Father" (John 13:1), He would pray to the Father to give them another Comforter so they would not be left comfortless. He told them, "The Comforter, which is the Holy Ghost, whom the Father will send in my name . . . shall teach you all things" (John 14:26).

Regarding the Holy Ghost, President Nelson taught, "He will bring thoughts to your mind which the Father and Son want you to receive. . . . He will bring a feeling of peace to your heart. He testifies of truth and will confirm what is truth as you hear and read the word of the Lord."[1]

This is why reading the Book of Mormon and the other standard works is so important. Many times when I've sought comfort or answers, exact words or phrases from the scriptures have entered my mind, followed by a feeling of peace. If I wasn't familiar with those scriptures, how would those answers or directions have come?

Elder Richard G. Scott stated, "We talk to God through prayer. He most often communicates back to us through His written word."[2]

Like Nephi experienced, when we are filled with the Spirit of the Lord, we also *feel* different and *act* differently.

One evening, I was engaged in a conversation with one of my teenage sons. We had been dealing with his frequent arguing, complaining, disrespect, and increasing unwillingness to attend church or participate in family activities. The conversation went round and round for close to an hour, with his arguments continuing. Finally, my son said he was done wasting his time talking to me. His obvious anger and negativity tore at my heart as I watched him leave the room, and I felt overwhelming discouragement, not knowing how to reach him. Eventually, I retreated to my own bedroom and shut the door.

A short time later, I heard a knock.

My son called out to me, asking to come in, his voice now calm. When he entered the room, his countenance was completely changed. Half laughing and half crying, he proceeded to apologize. He related that within minutes of leaving the room, specific scriptures he had studied in seminary came to his mind, and the Spirit humbled him, allowing him to clearly see his mistakes. He admitted he had been wrong.

Tears came to my eyes as I was overcome with gratitude to Heavenly Father. I felt His strength building my own, and I realized through this experience how much being filled with the Spirit can change hearts, sometimes almost instantaneously. The scripture in Ezekiel 36:26 rang with truth: "A new heart will I give you, and a new spirit will I put within you." Joy and hope filled my own heart for my son, who just a short time before seemed to be heading down a dark path. Inside, I rejoiced for the powerful lesson both of us learned that night.

As we seek to learn not only from seeing and hearing but also from feeling, especially through promptings from the Spirit, our capacity to learn and grow will expand. "Spiritual guidance is direction, enlightenment, knowledge, and motivation . . . from Jesus Christ through the Holy Spirit. It is personalized instruction adapted to your individual needs by One who understands them perfectly."[3]

Self-Reflection:
How does feeling the Spirit cause you to act differently?

3

TENDER MERCIES

"The tender mercies of the Lord are over all those whom he hath chosen, because of their faith, to make them mighty even unto the power of deliverance." (1 Nephi 1:20)

IN THE LAST VERSE OF CHAPTER 1 IN 1 NEPHI, NEPHI TELLS US HOW angry the people of Jerusalem were with his father, Lehi, after Lehi warned them of the destruction that was coming because of their wickedness. Then Nephi testified that the "tender mercies of the Lord" (1 Nephi 1:20) are over His people when they are faithful.

The Lord's tender mercies are personal and individualized. They don't occur randomly, nor are they merely coincidences, and their occurrence can strengthen our faith and reassure us that we are known and loved. They show up in different ways according to His perfect timing and can be in different forms. Tender mercies can be acknowledgment, blessings, reassurance, protection, directed guidance, an act of kindness, comfort, or an unexpected gift—all manifestations of the Lord's power and involvement in our lives.

When I was newly divorced, with my children in different stages of brokenness and hurt, the circumstances dictated that I move away from my neighborhood, ward, home, and friends that I had known and cared about for over twenty years. Through this challenging process, there were many days I barely recognized my life. Yet amidst all the heartache, change, and emotional ups and downs, I kept receiving reassurances to trust Heavenly Father. The Spirit reminded me to not give in to my fears and to keep listening, move forward, and believe it would all be okay.

Throughout this difficult upheaval, God gave me a tender mercy.

The home I was leaving had a beautiful rose garden that was very special to me. Each bush had been carefully chosen by size, color, and fragrance. Every summer, fresh roses filled my home and were lovingly shared with neighbors and friends. Leaving that rose garden when I moved was just something else I lost that compounded my sadness.

Heavenly Father knew.

The new home He led me to purchase after months of praying and searching had well-established pink rose bushes bordering the front walkway. It was a small thing, but I realized that because *I* cared about the roses, *He* did too.

Time passed and I remarried. Not long after, my husband, Trent, started receiving promptings that we needed to move out of state. It was not an easy decision, but we acted in faith. The home we purchased together had a large yard, and there was a particularly neglected area of it that was overgrown with morning glories. When I cleaned it out, I found a small rose bush hidden underneath. Once the space was opened, it had room to grow and blossom. Soon it had rosebuds.

I recognized that the *new* rosebush was another tender mercy from the Lord. He continued to be mindful of me, sending reassurances that He was with me in more changes in my life.

As wise Church leaders have taught, we can take comfort in knowing that "truly, for those with faithful hearts and eyes to see, the Lord's tender mercies are manifest amidst life's challenges."[1]

> ### *Self-Reflection:*
> *When have you experienced the Lord's tender mercies in your life?*

4

BLESSINGS OF OBEDIENCE

*"Blessed art thou, Nephi, because of thy faith. . . . And
inasmuch as ye shall keep my commandments, ye shall prosper."*
(1 Nephi 2:19–20)

IN THIS CHAPTER, LEHI RELATES A DREAM IN WHICH THE LORD
spoke to him and told him that "he should take his family and depart
into the wilderness" (1 Nephi 2:2). When Lehi told his wife and children that the Lord had asked them to do something difficult—leave
their home, friends, and precious things to travel into an unknown
wilderness—his family members were undoubtedly stunned and had
many feelings of their own regarding such a big change and sacrifice.

Young Nephi heard the complaints of his brothers regarding their
father's revelation, and he probably had a few doubts of his own, but
he sought and received personal spiritual confirmation that his father's
promptings were right. He said, "I did cry unto the Lord; and behold
he did visit me, and did soften my heart that I did believe all the
words which had been spoken by my father; wherefore, I did not rebel
against him like unto my brothers" (1 Nephi 2:16).

I love that Nephi shows us here that when we have questions
or doubts about something, we can take it to the Lord and get our
own answer and confirmation. Knowing for ourselves is much more

powerful than hearing it from another person. President Thomas S. Monson said, "In order for us to be strong and to withstand all the forces pulling us in the wrong direction, . . . we must have our own testimony."[1] Nephi needed to *know* in order to face all that was to come, and because he *knew*, he was able to face it faithfully.

The Lord told Nephi that he was "blessed because of [his] faith" (1 Nephi 2:19) and as he continued to be obedient to His commandments, he would prosper and be led to a land of promise. The Lord didn't, however, promise Nephi that it would be easy, and as we know from his record, it wasn't. But Nephi learned and testified that "the Lord giveth no commandments unto the children of men, save he shall prepare a way for them that they may accomplish the thing which he commandeth them" (1 Nephi 3:7).

The Lord doesn't promise *us* it will be easy either. But we are asked to remember "the blessed and happy state of those that keep the commandments of God. For behold, they are blessed in all things, both temporal and spiritual: and if they hold out faithful to the end they are received into heaven, that thereby they may dwell with God in a state of never-ending happiness . . . for the Lord God hath spoken it" (Mosiah 2:41).

To Trent and I, this means that even when things aren't easy, the blessings will come as we trust and follow the covenant path, and that we will have what we need in all aspects. For example, when we ended an unhealthy relationship causing turmoil in our lives and then acted with forgiveness, peace came and God brought others into our life to fill and overflow the void that the loss had caused. When we've been obedient to hard things God has asked us to do—like get married soon after we had both endured significant trauma, and move suddenly to a place where we knew no one before having employment lined up—God blessed us with courage and guided us step by step, confirming it was all His will. And when we've followed spiritual promptings to be generous with what we have by sharing it with others, God has sent greater abundance.

The Savior set the example of obedience when He said in the premortal Council in Heaven, "Father, thy will be done, and the glory be thine forever" (Moses 4:2). Throughout His ministry, He suffered all things, paid the price of our sins with His life, and taught us, "Come, follow me" (Luke 18:22).

"May we love Him so deeply and believe Him in faith so completely that we too obey, keep His commandments, and return to live with Him forever in the kingdom of our God."[2]

Self-Reflection:
What blessings have you experienced because of your obedience?

5

LED BY THE SPIRIT

"And I was led by the Spirit, not knowing beforehand the things which I should do. Nevertheless I went forth." (1 Nephi 4:6–7)

THE LORD SPOKE TO LEHI AGAIN IN A DREAM, COMMANDING THAT Nephi and his brothers should "return to Jerusalem . . . unto the house of Laban, and seek the records, and bring them down hither into the wilderness" (1 Nephi 3:2, 4). The "records," or brass plates, held the genealogy of his forefathers and the record of the Jews.

Unfortunately, their first two attempts at getting the records were unsuccessful.

They learned from an angelic visit that they needed to try again, and they were promised that this time, the Lord would deliver Laban into their hands. Still, Nephi's brothers doubted and murmured, but Nephi remained faithful. When darkness fell after they went back, he left his brothers in hiding and went into the city toward the house of Laban. He didn't know how he would accomplish the difficult task *this* time, especially after failing twice before, but he trusted in the guiding direction of the Spirit, acted anyway, and was "led by the Spirit" (1 Nephi 4:6).

Often in our lives, we don't have all the answers either. We may not know how things will work out when the direction isn't clear. The

Lord expects us to trust Him, pray, study the scriptures, and act in faith while continuing to move forward the best we can until we find clarity, guidance, or a roadblock directing us to change course.

Two faithful Russian Latter-day Saints, a man and a woman, had separately longed and sought for an eternal companion. After much sacrifice and saving to attend the temple, which was significantly far from his home, the man boarded a train en route. After getting settled in his seat, he saw a beautiful woman with a light-filled countenance sitting nearby. A prompting entered his thoughts that he should share the gospel with her. Not knowing for sure how to start, he pulled out his Book of Mormon and began to read, hoping she would notice. He didn't know she was already a member of the Church. At almost the same time, the woman received a similar prompting to share the gospel with the man and began reading in her own Book of Mormon.

When they both looked up simultaneously, they were astonished to see the Book of Mormon in the other's hands. This encounter on the train began their relationship, which led to them falling in love and being sealed in the temple for all eternity.[1]

Their willingness to act in faith, without knowing exactly why, allowed the Lord to guide and bless them.

"Our Father in Heaven knows His children's needs better than anyone else. It is His work and glory to help us at every turn, giving us marvelous temporal and spiritual resources to help us on our path to return to Him."[2]

Self-Reflection:
Do you willingly let the Lord lead you, even when the path forward isn't completely clear?

6

ESCAPE QUICKLY

*"And after I had traveled for the space of many hours in
darkness, I began to pray unto the Lord that he would have
mercy on me, according to the multitude of his tender mercies."*
(1 Nephi 8:8)

PRESIDENT NELSON ONCE GAVE A CONFERENCE TALK ABOUT THE
power of spiritual momentum, saying how one of our greatest challenges today is distinguishing between the truths of God and the
counterfeits of Satan. We know that Satan is our adversary and the
one "who spread[s] the works of darkness and abominations over all
the face of the land" (Helaman 6:28). He delights in our misery, but
we can cut it short by casting his influence out of our life—quickly!
The antidote to his scheme, according to President Nelson, is "daily
experiences worshipping the Lord and studying His gospel. . . . Give
Him a fair share of your time. As you do, notice what happens to your
positive spiritual momentum."[1]

I know that the faster I recognize Satan influencing me, and the
sooner I cast him out by literally commanding him to depart in the
name of Jesus Christ, the quicker my peace returns and the faster
I can feel an increase of light to counteract his darkness. Ongoing
prayer also gives me strength to thwart his relentless attacks. Reading

about the struggles of those in the Book of Mormon who also faced darkness can bring us comfort, reminding us that turning toward the Savior is always the right way.

One brother shared that Lehi's vision of the tree of life is one of his favorite stories in the Book of Mormon. One of the things he loves about this account is how it mentions that Lehi "traveled for the space of many hours in darkness" (1 Nephi 8:8) before he called upon the Lord to be rescued.

There have been several times in his life when he wandered in "darkness," but his testimony never faltered. He always knew the Church was true, including the Book of Mormon being the word of God and Joseph Smith being the prophet of the Restoration. However, there have been times when he has felt distant from the Spirit or questioned why he was experiencing certain trials.

During a particularly difficult time in his life when he was struggling with addiction, he slipped into a dark place. He felt lost and alone. This gave him an intimate knowledge that one of Satan's favorite tools is isolation. If he can get us on our own, he has a better chance of keeping us separated from the Lord, causing feelings of defeat and deceiving us to think there is no hope.

During this experience, this brother felt he was so unworthy that he couldn't reach out to the Lord in prayer. Forgiveness didn't feel like an option—he felt lower than dirt, and feeling so spiritually lost, he didn't know how to come back. This occurred while he was working with the youth in a church calling. Teaching Sunday lessons to them was one of the few times he felt like he had a tiny connection to the Spirit.

As he was preparing his upcoming lesson that week, the words in 1 Nephi 8:7–8 stuck out to him. They were highlighted from previous times he had read them, and he had written in the margin, "Call upon the Lord sooner to leave the darkness sooner." As soon as he read those words, he realized he too was traveling in darkness for "many hours" without calling upon the Lord to receive His tender mercies.

He reflected on what he needed to do.

He started praying again, asking what he needed to do to have the companionship of the Spirit again. He worked with his bishop, and his bishop helped him work through the repentance process. It was hard! He had to fight Satan's tactics of self-isolation every day, but as he continued to turn to the Savior, he felt renewed spiritual strength and the peace and joy that come only from truly repenting.

He has reflected often over this period of his life, realizing that if he would have turned to the Lord sooner, he would have felt peace and joy sooner. If he had worked on repenting, he would have saved himself months of traveling in spiritual darkness. He knows personally that the Lord will deliver us from darkness—in whatever form it may take—as long as we make the conscious decision to choose to turn and ask Him for help.

Self-Reflection:

Is there something you could change in your life by giving it to God more quickly?

7

HE KNOWS ALL

"The Lord knoweth all things from the beginning; wherefore, he prepareth a way to accomplish all his works among the children of men." (1 Nephi 9:6)

THE LORD COMMANDED NEPHI TO MAKE TWO SETS OF RECORDS. IN the larger set, he was to record the history of his people, mostly focusing on secular things. In the smaller set, he was to record his ministry, including sacred things. Nephi didn't know why the Lord requested this of him, but he trusted that it was "for a wise purpose" (1 Nephi 9:5), and he followed the Lord's directions obediently.

When we hold a physical copy of the Book of Mormon in our hands today, we can be reassured that the Lord knew exactly what He was doing when He gave Nephi that commandment. His plan to preserve the spiritual parts of Nephi's record blesses our lives every time we read and study from its pages and are spiritually fed. Every time the words bring us peace in a world of uncertainty and struggle, give us strength to face challenges, and prompt and guide us through personal revelation, we can know that God was in charge then—and that He is in charge now.

President Monson taught, "I never cease to be amazed by how the Lord can motivate and direct the length and breadth of His kingdom and yet have time to provide inspiration concerning one individual."[1]

God is in the details. And He knows what we, His children, need.

A sister felt this comfort and reminder from the Book of Mormon during a situation with her teenage daughter. She didn't realize how far off the rails things had gotten during the COVID-19 pandemic until her kids went back to school. Students were dressing very inappropriately and being asked to fill out forms about their preferred names and pronouns and whether it was okay for the teacher to use them in front of their parents.

This sister was angry and vocal about the school not enforcing their own dress code, but she didn't know there was even more going on—her daughter's theater teacher was having her class read foul and inappropriate plays. She thought her daughter was afraid to tell her for fear she would call her teacher and cause another scene.

But the Lord knew her situation, for He knows "all things from the beginning; wherefore he prepareth a way" (1 Nephi 9:6).

He *had* prepared in advance. A wonderful family moved in—just for the school year—with a teenage girl, Kayla, who also loved singing and drama and was in her daughter's theater class. Kayla told her mom what was going on, and her mom, who is sweet but also very direct and honest, called the theater teacher. She let her know she wasn't okay with the class materials, and the teacher changed course (as far as the foulness was concerned).

This teacher and many of the kids in the class continued to express worldly beliefs, but because Kayla was there, *her* daughter was protected spiritually.

Self-Reflection:
How have you noticed God in the details of your life?

8

LAMB OF GOD

"The Lamb of God is the Son of the Eternal Father, and the Savior of the world; . . . All men must come unto him, or they cannot be saved." (1 Nephi 13:40)

OVER THE NEXT SEVERAL CHAPTERS, NEPHI IS TAUGHT MANY THINGS by the Lord in vision. As I read these verses recently, I stopped on the words "Lamb of God" (1 Nephi 13:40) and began to do some research.

When Adam and Eve were cast out from the Garden of Eden, Heavenly Father gave them commandments to follow, including sacrificing lambs. An angel taught them that this was "in similitude of the sacrifice of the Only Begotten of the Father" (Moses 5:7) to remind them that they should do all things in the "name of the Son" (Moses 5:8), including repentance and prayer, so they could eventually return to God's presence.

In the Old Testament, the Lord directed Moses to institute the Passover. He commanded them to "take to them every man a lamb . . . without blemish, a male of the first year" (Exodus 12:5) and sacrifice it, with strict instructions of when and how to do it—in the evening on the fourteenth day of the first month at the temple, without any bones broken. The law also dictated how to cook the roasted flesh and where to mark its blood, symbolizing the sparing of their firstborn. Later, blood sacrifices were done away with.

In New Testament times, "looking up from water's edge, past the eager crowds seeking baptism at his hand, John, called the Baptist, saw in the distance his cousin, Jesus of Nazareth, striding resolutely toward him to make a request for the same ordinance. Reverently, but audible enough for those nearby to hear, John uttered . . . 'Behold the Lamb of God'"[1]

In the Gospel of John, we read that the Last Supper took place the day before Passover, which means the Savior could have been bound and crucified at the same time the Passover lambs were being sacrificed at the temple. It was also recorded that when the Jews complained to Pilate during the crucifixion that the three bodies could not remain on the crosses on the sabbath, the soldiers only broke the legs of the other men to hasten their death, but with Jesus, they pierced His side with a sword. "For these things were done, that the scripture should be fulfilled, A bone of him shall not be broken" (John 19:36). In similitude of the Passover lambs sacrificed without any broken bones, Jesus Christ, the Son of God and the purest of all, willingly sacrificed Himself for us.

In Him, our "faith" (Alma 7:14) and hope can be found "with [His] precious blood . . . as of a lamb without blemish" (1 Peter 1:19) that we may overcome Satan and be cleansed from all our sins through the grace of His Atonement.

"And every creature which is in heaven, and on the earth, and under the earth, and such as are in the sea, and all that are in them . . . [say], Blessing, and honour, and glory, and power, be unto him that sitteth upon the throne, and unto the Lamb for ever and ever" (Revelation 5:14).

I love how this scripture in 1 Nephi helped me dig deeper to understand and learn the background and historical significance of Christ's title as the Lamb of God. In all the other times I read this, I never took the time to grasp it in this way. This was a clear example to me of how each time we read the Book of Mormon, we can be enlightened in new ways.

Self-Reflection:
What other titles of Jesus Christ stand out to you?

9

IRON ROD: WORD OF GOD

"It was the word of God; and whoso would hearken unto the word of God, and would hold fast unto it, they would never perish; neither could the temptations and the fiery darts of the adversary overpower them unto blindness, to lead them away to destruction." (1 Nephi 15:24)

IN THIS CHAPTER, NEPHI CONTINUES TO BE TAUGHT BECAUSE OF HIS desire to know the things Lehi had seen. Because he exercised faith, he was "caught away in the Spirit of the Lord" (1 Nephi 11:1) and shown many things, including the tree of life and it's interpretation. After his vision ended, he returned to his father's tent where he found his brothers arguing about the things their father had told them.

Nephi asked, "Have ye inquired of the Lord?" (1 Nephi 15:8).

They replied that they had not.

Nephi gave them wise counsel about having faith and diligently keeping the commandments. Then, in response to their questions, he started sharing with them what he had learned. He explained that the rod of iron their father saw leading to the tree of life represented the "word of God" (1 Nephi 15:24).

Modern and ancient prophets have given us much counsel on the importance of learning and knowing the word of God from the scriptures. This essential spiritual nourishment will fortify and arm us "with the Spirit so [we] can resist evil, hold fast to the good, and find joy in this life."[1] As we study and "meditate . . . day and night . . . [observing] to do according to all that is written" (Joshua 1:8) and listen to the whisperings of the Spirit, we will "prosper exceedingly" (2 Nephi 5:13). We will also find success in what matters most; know what we should do in all things; find healing, peace, and hope; and be made "wise unto salvation" (2 Timothy 3:15).

The world we live in is full of conflicting ideas, doctrines, principles, and what many incorrectly call "truth." The Savior Himself taught from the Mount of Olives a discourse in which he warned against deception and false prophets. He said, "Whoso treasureth up my word, shall not be deceived" (Joseph Smith—Matthew 1:37).

When Nephi's brothers told him they hadn't inquired of the Lord themselves for help in understanding Lehi's words, Nephi asked, "How is it you do not keep the commandments of the Lord? How is it that ye will perish because of the hardness of your hearts? Do ye not remember the things which the Lord hath said?—If you will not harden your hearts and ask me in faith, believing that you shall receive . . . surely these things will be made known unto you" (1 Nephi 15:10).

It's the same for each of us.

In order to understand and hearken unto the word of God, our hearts need to be soft. This is how we hear Him. When hearts are hard, the Spirit withdraws. When hearts are soft and sensitive, it is easier to be humble, submissive, gentle, meek, full of patience and long-suffering, loving toward others and ourselves, and more diligent in keeping the commandments.

This is illustrated in a story about a sister who became involved in a disagreement with a relative over a political issue. During their conversation, in front of other family members, the relative thoroughly picked apart the sister's knowledge and comments, determined to prove her wrong. The contention this created let loose the "fiery darts of the adversary" (1 Nephi 15:24), which caused the sister to feel uninformed and foolish.

That night as she knelt to pray, she told Heavenly Father what had happened, why she was upset, and how difficult she felt her relative was. At one point during her prayer conversation, she paused and then with surprise said, "You probably want me to love her."

Love her?

She continued her prayer, inquiring, "How can I love her? I don't think I even like her. My heart is hard—my feelings are hurt. I can't do it."

Then a new thought came, surely from the Spirit. She said, "But *You* love her, Heavenly Father." Then she asked, "Would You give me a portion of Your love for her, so I can love her too?"

Gradually her feelings began to soften and her heart began to change. This helped her see her relative differently and sense the real value she had in Heavenly Father's eyes.

Studying God's word in the scriptures brought further understanding. She found comfort in the words of Isaiah, who said, "The Lord bindeth up the breach of his people, and healeth the stroke of their wound" (Isaiah 30:26).

As time passed, the gap between her and her relative sweetly closed, and she experienced personal healing. She also learned that even if her relative didn't accept her change of heart, she could turn to God for help, for "Heavenly Father will help us love even those we may think are unlovable, if we plead for His aid."[2]

Self-Reflection:
How has holding on to the "iron rod" helped you?

10

IMPERFECT YET "CHOSEN"

"And it came to pass that I, Nephi, beheld the pointers
which were in the ball, that they did work according to the
faith and diligence and heed which we did give unto them."
(1 Nephi 16:28)

ONE NIGHT, AFTER LEHI AND HIS FAMILY HAD BEEN LIVING IN THE valley of Lemuel for a while, the Lord told Lehi that the next day it would be time to leave and journey into the wilderness. When he got up in the morning and opened the door of his tent, "to his great astonishment he beheld upon the ground a ball of curious workmanship" (1 Nephi 16:10). He discovered that it was a director or compass of sorts—a Liahona—presumably put there by the Lord to guide them on their way,

After everyone gathered the things they needed for their journey—personal belongings, provisions, seeds, and tents—they departed. They followed "the directions of the ball, which led them to more fertile parts of the wilderness" (1 Nephi 16:16) near the borders of the Red Sea.

It wasn't long before problems arose—something that inevitably occurs for everyone in the journey of life—and they found themselves without adequate food. Their hunger and fatigue caused great murmuring amongst themselves and against the Lord. While they struggled in this state, the Liahona didn't work the way it had worked before, and they didn't know where to go to find food. This trial made them realize that the pointers in the Liahona worked "according to the faith and diligence and heed which [they] did give unto them" (1 Nephi 16:28). This experience taught them humility and increased their understanding of obedience, even when things are hard. They also learned about the Lord's mercy and how He blesses us when we repent.

Nephi recorded, "I, Nephi, did go forth up into the top of the mountain, according to the directions which were given upon the ball . . . that I did obtain food for our families. And . . . how great was [our] joy! And it came to pass [we] did humble [ourselves] before the Lord, and did give thanks unto him" (1 Nephi 16:30–32).

We can relate this story of an imperfect yet "chosen" family to ourselves. Just as the Lord commanded them to leave their home in Jerusalem and travel in the wilderness toward a "land of promise," so too He has commanded us to travel in this wilderness of mortality, continually journeying toward God's promised blessings.

One brother shared the following thoughts:

> I am relieved to know that even a family as amazing as this—even a people who are memorialized for all time in the holy scriptures—have such obvious and blatant shortcomings as do any of us who are alive today.
>
> Knowing that this family was "mostly" faithful, and that they truly did desire to follow the Lord above all else . . . yet seeing how many times they come up short (and still repent, and turn back to the Lord) . . . That knowledge brings me peace and hope in my own life as I struggle to follow the Lord and also find myself so many times coming up so short.
>
> [God] knows us so well that He can look beyond our failings and see our potential and our talents and our capacity as His children to help Him accomplish His work.
>
> I am relieved to know that even the men and women in our holy scripture were still *just* mortal men and women, and that I don't *have* to be perfect to be accepted by God. I only have to believe and be willing to always give Him my best.[1]

President Dieter F. Uchtdorf reassures us, "Though we are incomplete, God loves us completely. Though we are imperfect, He loves us perfectly. Though we may feel lost and without compass, God's love encompasses us completely."[2]

It's comforting to know that it's okay for us to be on an up-and-down journey of growth that occurs over time, and that "time" doesn't look the same for everyone. The statement "A saint is a sinner that keeps trying"[3] should feel reassuring—I know it does for Trent and me.

Self-Reflection:
How have you felt the Lord's mercy?

11

RAW MEAT MOMENTS

"And so great were the blessings of the Lord upon us, that while we did live upon raw meat in the wilderness, our women did give plenty of suck for their children, and were strong, yea, even like unto the men; and they began to bear their journeyings without murmurings." (1 Nephi 17:2)

DURING THE TIME LEHI'S FAMILY JOURNEYED IN THE WILDERNESS, the women bore children. But despite the difficult living conditions they experienced, the Lord was with them. They were blessed with strength, and their babies had what they needed to thrive.

A sister missionary shared the following experience.

Her sweet mom often refers to this verse, 1 Nephi 17:2, during difficult times. Sometimes when we pray, God will deliver us from our trials, like when an angel appeared to stop the violence of Laman and Lemuel toward Nephi and Sam earlier in their story (see 1 Nephi 3:29). But oftentimes, it seems we have "raw meat" moments instead.

God could have delivered something miraculous to Lehi's family, such as a fire for them to cook their meat with, or bread to eat like Elijah. But instead, the miracle He performed was not on the food but on the strength of those who were eating the raw meat. It's especially powerful because these women were nursing, and their proper nutrition was vital. Because they relied on the Lord, they became strong "even like unto the men" (1 Nephi 17:2), even though they were in completely unfavorable circumstances.

God did not ease the *burden*—He strengthened the *carrier* of the burden.

She often thinks about this verse while enduring trials, and she strives to call upon God to strengthen her during her "raw meat moments."

God has a plan for each of us, and He knows what needs to be accomplished in our lives for us to grow into our full potential. And through our trials, as we trust Him, we can be refined "to bear [our] journeyings without murmurings" (1 Nephi 17:2).

God can see the whole picture when we can't. An illustration of seeing things in the proper perspective was told about the sculptor Michelangelo: "As [he] was chiseling a block of marble, a boy came every day and watched shyly. When the figure of David emerged and appeared from that stone, complete for all the world to admire, the boy asked Michelangelo, 'How did you know he was in there?'"[1]

Michelangelo's perspective as an artist was different from the boy's perspective, who watched his masterpiece emerge from raw stone. God's vision of what we can become may be different from our own. He tells us, "As the heavens are higher than the earth, so are my ways higher than your ways, and my thoughts higher than your thoughts" (Isaiah 55:9).

> **Self-Reflection:**
> *Is your perspective aligned with God's perspective?*

12

HE WILL HELP US

"And I said unto them: If God had commanded me to do all things I could do them. If he should command me that I should say unto this water, be thou earth, it should be earth; and if I should say it, it would be done. And now, if the Lord has such great power, and has wrought so many miracles among the children of men, how is it that he cannot instruct me, that I should build a ship?" (1 Nephi 17:50–51)

LEHI'S FAMILY CONTINUED THEIR JOURNEY IN THE WILDERNESS. Despite facing many afflictions, they were blessed by the Lord as they obeyed His commandments. After traveling eight years, they came to a land called Bountiful near a sea they called Irreantum. There the Lord instructed Nephi that he needed to build a ship to carry them to the promised land. Nephi had many questions about how this could be accomplished, especially since he had no tools. The Lord addressed all his concerns and gave him instructions on how to proceed.

His brothers didn't want to labor on this huge project, and they complained and mocked him for thinking he could actually build the ship. The hardness of their hearts made Nephi sorrowful, which caused his brothers to rejoice, thinking they had convinced him he couldn't do it. Their taunting included them saying that just like their father, he was being led by "foolish imaginations of his heart" (1 Nephi 17:20).

Nephi talked with them about many things, including the history of their fathers, reminding them what happens to those who are wicked and how the Lord blesses those who are righteous. As he anguished over his brothers' hard hearts, the Spirit of God filled him, protecting him from their increasing anger at his words. Nephi then testified, "If God had commanded me to do all things I could do them" (1 Nephi 17:50).

I love his faith and example!

On numerous occasions throughout my life, I've felt prompted or guided to do something that hasn't felt easy. When I've hesitated and doubted my lack of knowledge or ability to proceed, the adversary wastes no time in playing on those fears and causing them to grow. But like Nephi, I've learned that as I exercise faith, even if that faith starts small, then God will help me do what He asks of me. And He has—each and every time.

One sister felt the Lord guiding her in many areas of her life. She learned that trusting the guidance you receive is more than simply saying, "Yes, I will obey." It involves action, which often seems very hard. She hadn't ever intended to go on a mission, but the Lord had a different plan for her. Serving a mission taught her to love all of God's children, and it became one of the greatest experiences of her life.

Attending a university wasn't easy, and after failing a few papers and struggling with studying, she thought it wasn't for her. She received gentle promptings three times to go back before she finally listened and obeyed. There she learned about entrepreneurship. She also learned to be more observant, creative, passionate, and proactive. Through her research, she was also led to people she needed to meet and learn from and eventually got a degree in arts and commerce.

Later she was led to start her own business, and once again she found herself doing something she never thought she would. She never saw herself as someone leading in that way, but the Lord had other ideas. Before she officially started the business, she prayed to God, sharing how she was feeling. She received an answer from the Holy Ghost: "God knows that you will always do what He asks of you. He trusts you." Whenever she goes through hard times, she is reminded of that moment and knows she must keep moving forward.

She said, "When the Lord asks you to do something hard, do it! You'll be surprised at what you are capable of under His perfect guidance and mercy."[1]

Self-Reflection:
Are you willing to do whatever God asks of you?

13

BE STILL AND KNOW

"And it came to pass that I prayed unto the Lord; and after I prayed the winds did cease, and the storm did cease, and there was great calm." (1 Nephi 18:21)

AFTER THE SHIP WAS BUILT, NEPHI WROTE THAT THEY "DID ALL GO down into the ship, with our wives and our children" (1 Nephi 18:6). This group included Jacob and Joseph, the two younger brothers who had been born to Lehi and Sariah in the wilderness. They loaded the ship with their provisions and the things the Lord directed them to take, and then they set sail. After they had been at sea for many days, Laman and Lemuel, the sons of Ishmael, and their wives began to party, dance, sing, and get caught up in much rudeness.

Nephi was afraid their behavior would anger the Lord. When he voiced his concerns, they became angry with him and tied him with cords. This caused the Liahona to stop working. A great storm arose, and the ship was driven back and tossed on the troubled sea. On the fourth day, as the tempest continued to rage, and after ignoring the pleadings of their parents and other family members, "the power of God which threatened them with destruction" (1 Nephi 18:20) finally softened their hearts. They then repented and untied Nephi. In his hands, the compass started to work again, and faithfully, despite great physical pain, he "prayed unto the Lord" for the storm to end. After his prayer, "the storm did cease, and there was great calm" (1 Nephi 18:21).

The Lord heard Nephi's prayer, and it was answered. He also hears *our* prayers when we are "tossed about" by figurative storms on our own seas of life.

In the world we live in, peace can be fleeting or elusive. Contention, wars, violence, natural disasters, and shifting economies can all create struggle. Other threats are more personal—depression, anxiety, addiction, pain, debt, sickness, conflict in relationships, unemployment, loneliness, and more can also create turmoil. But as we turn to the Savior to answer our prayers for "deliverance," we can know that His timing is always perfect.

Today isn't the whole story.

We can isolate ourselves and stare at the storm, focusing on its darkness, giving in to fear, shaking with the cold and wind, feeling hopeless and alone, like in Matthew 8:24: "And behold, there arose a great tempest in the sea, insomuch the ship was covered with the waves. . . . And his disciples came to him . . . saying, Lord, save us: we perish." *Or* we can choose to listen and embrace the truth that comes from God, trust Him, and learn what He wants us to learn. As the Savior said in Matthew 8:26: "Why are ye fearful, O ye of little faith? Then he arose, and rebuked the winds and the sea; and there was a great calm."

Sometimes, His way doesn't involve immediately calming the storm. Instead, He calms *us* by giving us more strength to endure while we grow from the experience. He wants us to trust Him, "be still, and know" (Psalm 46:10) that He is there.

Self-Reflection:
Remember, if today seems too hard, hang on! Today isn't the end of the story. Can you think of three things you are grateful for? Write them down!

PART II

THE SECOND BOOK
OF NEPHI
(ABOUT 588–545 BC)

*"The truths of the Book of Mormon
have the power to heal, comfort,
restore, succor, strengthen, console,
and cheer our souls."*

—President Russell M. Nelson[1]

14

"CONSECRATE THINE AFFLICTIONS"

"Nevertheless, Jacob, my firstborn in the wilderness, thou knowest the greatness of God; and he shall consecrate thine afflictions for thy gain." (2 Nephi 2:2)

LEHI AND HIS FAMILY ARRIVE AT THE PROMISED LAND AFTER THEY had "sailed for the space of many days" (1 Nephi 18:23) and begin to settle there—planting seeds, finding beasts in the forests for their needs, and discovering ore, gold, silver, and copper. As Lehi's life draws to an end, he prophesies and talks to his family about what they have gone through, saying how "merciful the Lord had been in warning us that we should flee from the land of Jerusalem. For, behold . . . I have seen in a vision . . . that Jerusalem is destroyed" (2 Nephi 1:3–4), and "notwithstanding our afflictions, we have obtained a land of promise, a land which is choice above all other lands" (2 Nephi 1:5). He shares things of the Spirit, teaches his sons about obedience, and encourages them to put on the armor of righteousness, and then he addresses each of them one by one.

Chapter 2 begins with Lehi counseling his son Jacob, "my first-born in the days of my tribulation in the wilderness. And behold, in thy childhood thou hast suffered afflictions and much sorrow, because of the rudeness of thy brethren. Nevertheless . . . thou knowest the greatness of God; and he shall consecrate thine afflictions for thy gain" (2 Nephi 2:1–2).

The teaching and wisdom that Lehi passes down are not only important for Jacob but also for each of us. As it is with many prophets and their written words in the scriptures, their teachings have a great impact on those who read them. And as we apply their teachings, we can dig deeper.

For example, to *consecrate* means to make or declare sacred.[1] So how does someone declare their afflictions sacred? How does someone take the pain, sorrow, regret, or current tempest in their life—when they feel like they can't even breathe—and make it sacred?

Some of the challenges in my life have included multiple job losses, addiction, bankruptcy, teenagers, depression, suicidal thoughts, illness, and the death of a spouse. Although this is not an exhaustive list, it is representative of a list that can be identified with.

With trials like these, there were two directions I could head. One was to turn away from God and choose the world's ways of coping and medicating. The other way was to turn toward God and try to understand how to learn, grow, and consecrate the affliction—making the affliction sacred for my gain.

One way to describe this is by noting the difference between pride and humility. The world would have me rely on myself through any possible means for support. But I know that this increases pride—pride in my ability to deal, process, overcome, or "white-knuckle it" through on my own strength or through the resources of my wealth and position. Pride is defined as enmity toward God and toward our fellowmen. Enmity means hatred toward, hostility to, or a state of opposition.[2] This does not line up with consecrating or turning my afflictions into something that can make me holier.

The opposite of pride is humility—"becoming humble, meek, submissive, patient, full of love and all long-suffering" (Alma 13:28). By doing this, the Lord can bring me to a better understanding of the Atonement of His Son and the Savior Jesus Christ. I have decided that my favorite way to consecrate my afflictions is with meekness. Elder David A. Bednar defines meekness, saying that it's "a defining attribute of the Redeemer and is distinguished by righteous responsiveness, willing submissiveness, and strong self-restraint."[3]

I believe that coming to the altar of the Lord in humility and meekness is the way to receive heavenly gain.

> *Self-Reflection:*
> *What is your favorite definition of humility and meekness?*

15

THIS IS RIGHTEOUSNESS

"For it must needs be, that there is an opposition in all things. If not so, my firstborn in the wilderness, righteousness could not be brought to pass, neither wickedness, neither holiness nor misery, neither good nor bad. Wherefore, all things must needs be a compound in one." (2 Nephi 2:11)

JACOB WAS NOT BORN IN THE LUXURY OF JERUSALEM. HE DID NOT know the lifestyle of his parents and four older brothers. He was born and lived in the wilderness as his family struggled to survive. His experience was unique compared to his brothers. The same is true for each of us.

Individual challenges and the opposition in our lives are unique. Yes, someone else has likely experienced similar opposition as you, but you are the one facing it now! That makes the opposition yours *and* your opportunity. You can hate it and go it alone, or you can help bring about righteousness.

One brother reflected on this scripture about there being "opposition in all things" (2 Nephi 2:11). He described that one common escape from facing a present challenge is the feeling of numbness. Feeling numb allows a person to go through each day with an emptiness that covers them like a shroud. The humanity through connectedness in others is almost forgotten as they're just trying to survive each day. But in the deadness of the mind and soul not functioning as one, there is an opportunity to find righteousness. In the same space where this brother felt nothing, he discovered the choice to turn his heart and mind to God instead.

Then he makes the choice to *feel*.

It may come as sorrow, sadness, and disappointment. However, when it shows up as joy, it is like life being shot back into his soul. The feeling of humanity is restored again. To him, this is a testimony of the need for opposition. He prizes the joy so much more because of so many shed tears. This is a moment of redemption when he feel wholeness restored and knows that God is in the details of his life.

To him, this is "righteousness."

Self-Reflection:
When you feel joy return after sorrow, how does that feel to you?

16

Heavenly GPS

"Adam fell that man might be; and men are, that they might have joy." (2 Nephi 2:25)

Lehi's incredible counsel to Jacob continues with this expression of what we as God's children are meant to feel as we navigate this mortal existence.

A sister heard the Lord's voice as she studied and contemplated this scripture. She thought about how GPS systems are used by many people in today's world to help them travel to their destinations, and she suggests that we use our internal GPS system to help us find true "joy" (2 Nephi 2:25), noting how *GPS* could stand for *gratitude, patience*, and *service*.

Gratitude is her go-to when she is feeling down. We have so many things to be thankful for. As it states in a popular hymn, "Count your many blessings; name them one by one, / And it will surprise you what the Lord has done."[1]

She proposes that a great way to keep blessings close to our hearts is to record them in a gratitude journal. She has been recording positive thoughts in a journal for many years. One of her favorite activities is to go back and read what she has written in the past. This simple act of reading these pages always brings joy to her heart.

Patience is next.

King Benjamin encourages us to become as a little child and be "submissive, meek, humble, patient, full of love, willing to submit to all things which the Lord seeth fit to inflict upon him, even as a child submits to his father" (Mosiah 3:19).

When we are going through a tough trial, it is easy to blame our situation on anyone except ourselves, even the Lord. Rarely do we hear people take responsibility for their current situation or hear people say they are enjoying the trials they currently have. But we do hear many times how great the trial was when it's finished. Only after going through a trial do we learn the lessons the Lord wants us to learn.

He knows our situation much better than we do—we just need to be patient and see where the experience takes us, doing all we can to get through it. That's how we learn the lessons we need to learn. She is surprised by how much joy she can feel in her life when she is working through trials. As she is patient and understanding, she builds a partnership with the Lord. There is much "joy" in that.

And lastly, *service.*

Giving service to others helps us put our own struggles on the back burner. Our problems seem fewer when we are actively serving others. The service we give can be as small or as large as we want to make it. A complimentary note on Facebook Messenger, a letter in the mail, or a phone call to say something nice to someone can work wonders in building up their spirits as well as our own. Often all we need to do is drop something on someone's doorstep anonymously or simply ask someone how they're doing.

Her friend heard Sister Sharon Eubank give a talk on service[2] and was inspired to help her son fix up their home. With many people helping with both time and money, they renovated the kitchen, dining room, and living room in one day. Tears come to her eyes every time she thinks of this. She is grateful the gospel teaches that serving one another helps us in our journey home to return to Heavenly Father.

Have you ever seen a priesthood holder put his hands on his own head and give himself a blessing? No, someone else is there to give them a blessing when they need it. As we serve one another, we experience much joy and build solid relationships with others.

President Nelson has taught, "Life is filled with detours and dead ends, trials and challenges of every kind. Each of us has likely had times when distress, anguish, and despair almost consumed us. Yet we are here to have joy? Yes! The answer is a resounding yes! But how is that possible? And what must we do to claim the joy that Heavenly Father has in store for us? . . . Saints can be happy under every circumstance. We can feel joy even while having a bad day, a bad week, or even a bad year!"[3]

As we have *gratitude* for what we have, *patience* as we go through the trials of life, and give *service* to others so that our trials don't consume us, we find that life is truly full of joy!

Self-Reflection:
How can you be more grateful, patient, and focused on serving others?

17

THE CHOICE

"Wherefore, men are free according to the flesh; and all things are given them which are expedient unto man. And they are free to choose liberty and eternal life, through the great Mediator of all men, or to choose captivity and death, according to the captivity and power of the devil; for he seeketh that all men might be miserable like unto himself." (2 Nephi 2:27)

THE LAST VERSE I WANT TO SHARE FROM THIS INSPIRING CHAPTER OF instruction from Lehi to his son Jacob has to do with choice. We have a choice to have "liberty" or "captivity," "eternal life" or "death" (2 Nephi 2:27). When stated like this, it seems that the choice would be easy for everyone to make, yet it's not. Doing so requires understanding what agency is and then choosing to do not *your* will but *His*.

About ten years ago when I was preparing for my first marathon, I embarked on and completed many long runs. The runs increased in distance, building my stamina, strength, and endurance. On my sixth planned run (out of eight), my goal was a distance of nineteen miles. While I ran, I listened to my favorite motivational speaker, Elder Neal A. Maxwell. I love my "Brother Neal." I learned early on in my running journey that listening to apostles was far superior to music or contemporary podcasts as I pushed my body mile after mile.

At the ninth mile on this particular run, I listened to my "Brother Neal" say, "The submission of one's will is really the only uniquely personal thing we have to place on God's altar. The many other things we 'give,' brothers and sisters, are actually the things He has already given or loaned to us. However, when you and I finally submit ourselves, by letting our individual wills be swallowed up in God's will, then we are really giving something to Him! It is the only possession which is truly ours to give!"[1] As I heard these words through my earbuds, I was struck by the Spirit and for the first time truly understood what this meant. I understood deeply Christ's words, "Not my will, but thine, be done" (Luke 22:42).

Up until this point in my life, I had never considered that the only thing I could ever give Jesus was my agency, doing what Christ would have me do. When I realized this, I started to openly weep while I ran on the side of the road, tears of understanding mixed with the sweat of my brow, the sobbing from my body syncing with the constant movement of placing one foot in front of the other.

I thought of the cars driving by seeing me in this state and thinking to themselves that I must really be in a lot of running pain. Little did they know that my life was being changed. I would come to realize that this experience would be one of my life's biggest changing moments—a pivotal turning point that came from understanding where I wanted to go and who I wanted to follow: Jesus Christ.

"Being a disciple of Jesus Christ is not just one of many things we do. The Savior is the motivating power behind *all* that we do. He is not a rest stop in our journey. He is not a scenic byway or even a major landmark. He is 'the way, the truth, and the life: no man cometh unto the Father, but by [Jesus Christ].' That is the Way and our ultimate destination."[2]

Self-Reflection:
Are you willing to give your agency back to God?

18

DELIGHT AND PONDER

"Behold, my soul delighteth in the things of the Lord; and my heart pondereth continually upon the things which I have seen and heard." (2 Nephi 4:16)

EARLY IN THIS CHAPTER, NEPHI LOSES HIS FATHER LEHI TO DEATH. Despite Laman, Lemuel, and the sons of Ishmael being upset with him because of the warnings and counsel from the Lord, Nephi rejoiced in the Lord and His ways. One of the ways he did this was through pondering or meditating.

My favorite lesson taught about meditation comes from a general conference address back in 1967:

Meditation leads to spiritual communion with God through the Holy Spirit. We pay too little attention to the value of meditation, a principle of devotion. In our worship there are two elements: One is spiritual communion arising from our own meditation; the other, instruction from others, particularly from those who have authority to guide and instruct us. Of the two, the more profitable introspectively is the meditation. Meditation is the language of the soul. It is defined as "a form of private devotion, or spiritual exercise, consisting in deep, continued reflection on some religious theme." Meditation is a form of prayer. . . .

Meditation is one of the most secret, most sacred doors through which we pass into the presence of the Lord. Jesus set the example for us. As soon as he was baptized and received the Father's approval, "This is my Beloved Son, in whom I am well pleased" (Matthew 3:17), Jesus [went] to what is now known as the mount of temptation. I like to think of it as the mount of meditation where, during the forty days of fasting, he communed with himself and his Father, and contemplated upon the responsibility of his great mission. One result of this spiritual communion was such strength as enabled him to say to the tempter:

"Get thee hence, Satan: for it is written, Thou shalt worship the Lord thy God, and him only shalt thou serve" (Matt. 4:10).[1]

I love that. He says that in worship, there are two elements. One is instruction from inspired leaders (those in authority), and the second is meditation. Of the two, meditation is more important. Think about that!

Diony had thoughts about this scripture too. She shared the following experience:

As I read 2 Nephi 4:16, I could feel Nephi's joy in the goodness of God despite the recent and painful loss of his father, and my own heart filled with love for the Lord for all the ways He has taught and blessed me. The burdens and cares I was carrying right then felt lifted from my heart while I pondered these feelings as I studied that day, and I wanted to shout, "I glory in my Jesus" (2 Nephi 33:6)! It was another tangible reminder to me that the more I ponder, meditate, and seek, the more knowledge and understanding I receive about my purpose and the closer to Him I become. Doing this—reading in order to truly hear Him—is bringing greater light into my life and more peace, which counteracts affliction and the darkness in the world that too often presses in.

Self-Reflection:
When is the last time you meditated? What did you learn?

19

TRUST HIM IN WEAKNESS

"I am encompassed about, because of the temptations and the sins which do so easily beset me. And when I desire to rejoice, my heart groaneth because of my sins; nevertheless, I know in whom I have trusted. . . . And by day have I waxed bold in mighty prayer before him; yea, my voice have I sent up on high; and angels came down and ministered unto me."
(2 Nephi 4:18–19, 24)

AFTER LEHI'S DEATH, NEPHI RECOUNTS THE PRIESTHOOD BLESSINGS that Lehi had given to their family before he returned to his eternal home. Nephi's brothers (Laman, Lemuel, and the sons of Ishmael) were angry with Nephi "because of the admonitions of the Lord" (2 Nephi 4:13), which he was "constrained to speak unto them, according to his word" (2 Nephi 4:14).

As Nephi pondered the things he has seen and heard, he felt and expressed sorrow because of the weaknesses of his flesh, saying, "My heart groaneth because of my sins; nevertheless, I know in whom I have trusted" (2 Nephi 4:19). He also expressed how he knows God hears his prayers, teaches him in visions during the night, and sends down angels to minister unto him.

As one sister read this passage about Nephi sorrowing because of his sins and temptations, she felt the Spirit teach her that we actually are *blessed* to have weaknesses. One of her weaknesses is anxiety. She believes she has a lot of trust in the Lord, but she also realizes that trusting Him doesn't always mean He takes the trial away. Because of her anxiety, she finds herself pleading with the Lord more often than not for His help to cope. And like Nephi, she too has felt angels come down and minister to her, lift her up, and help her move confidently forward.

Another sister was struggling about halfway through her mission with their ward mission leader. After several negative interactions, she and her companion approached the bishop. She hoped his solution would be to talk with the ward mission leader and fix the problem. The counsel she received instead was that she was being prideful and overly critical. She left feeling very misunderstood and frustrated. As she vented to her companion, a scripture phrase entered her thoughts: "The guilty taketh the truth to be hard" (1 Nephi 16:2). Her pride may have prevented her from accepting the bishop's chastisement, but could she really argue with the Holy Ghost as well?

This humbling experience helped her understand she needed to be honest with herself and her flaws. She learned that if her weaknesses and shortcomings remain obscured in the shadows, then the redeeming power of the Savior cannot heal them and make them strengths. However, if she is brave enough to be vulnerable and admit her weaknesses in humility, God can help her turn them into strengths through His grace.

After all, honestly acknowledging our weaknesses—or seeing ourselves as we truly are—is the first step on the path to positive change. As she continues to be honest and seek guidance from the Spirit, her Heavenly Father will help her know what needs to change in her life. And as she relies on Jesus Christ, His Atonement, and His refining power, she will see improvement in herself.

Although it was unpleasant to admit her mistakes in that moment of chastisement, she knows that when she chooses to be humble and honest with herself and with God, she is happier and more accepting of herself. She knows that despite her flaws, she is of divine worth to her Heavenly Father—but He still wants her to improve. Through the power of His Son, Jesus Christ, and sincere repentance, she can become so much better than she ever dreamed she could be.[1]

I know that as we let ourselves be vulnerable in our weakness, we can feel God's divine influence in the face of adversity and trust Him in our opportunities to grow.

Self-Reflection:
What can you be vulnerable about—and with whom—
to accomplish the will of the Lord?

20

FORGIVING YOURSELF

"Awake, my soul! No longer droop in sin. Rejoice, O my heart, and give place no more for the enemy of my soul."
(2 Nephi 4:28)

I LOVE THE FOURTH CHAPTER OF 2 NEPHI. I FEEL LIKE MY HEART AND soul connect to it on so many levels. Some of my favorite things about it come at the end with Nephi's declaration of forgiveness, specifically forgiveness to himself. The way the chapter concludes, with a powerful prayer to the Lord, teaches how close to God we can become through prayer—especially during repentance.

When Nephi testified that "God will give liberally to him that asketh" (2 Nephi 4:35), this shows his great faith in the process. For many people, including myself, the concept and action of forgiving oneself is hard. But I've learned from experience that if it's done regularly and consistently, it becomes more natural.

I implemented this during a time of my life when I was in the grips of addiction. As I attended addiction recovery meetings, I learned about seeking forgiveness in step 8 of the 12-step program, which involves writing down a list of those you have harmed throughout your life. While in an addiction recovery meeting, I learned that in addition to those you have actively harmed in your life, consider that there are no secrets in heaven—that harmony and love abound. As brothers and sisters of the same heavenly parents, we are all to be there together, and there are no corners where those you don't want to associate with will congregate or isolate in groups. Instead, everybody will be unified. Think of anyone that you are embarrassed, uncomfortable, or ashamed around for any reason, and put their name on your list too—now is the time to be a peacemaker.

In the addiction recovery program manual, it expounds on step 8, Seeking Forgiveness:

> Finally, after you have listed everyone you have harmed, add one more name to the list—your own. When you indulged in your addictions [throughout your life], you harmed yourself as well as others.
>
> As you work [on this step], remember that step 8 is not an exercise in casting guilt or shame on anyone—either yourself or those on your lists. The Savior will lift the burdens of guilt and shame as you take one more honest look at troubles in your relationships and your part in them. By becoming willing to make amends, you benefit from the peace of knowing that Heavenly Father is pleased with your efforts. This step helps you take the actions that enable the Savior to set you free from your past.[1]

Understanding that forgiveness applies to myself just as much as to others has had a profound effect on my life. There are times now that when the natural man in me expresses his opinion or says something hurtful, my spiritual man recognizes what has happened immediately. I often sincerely apologize instantly, and in that process, I forgive myself for the error in my interaction. Others then can either receive or reject my apology or wait to accept it later. This choice to forgive myself and choose immediate repentance brings me closer to Jesus Christ. This did not come easily, but over many years of conscious effort, it came.

"That great morning of forgiveness may not come at once. Do not give up if at first you fail. Often the most difficult part of repentance is to forgive yourself. Discouragement is part of that test. Do not give up. That brilliant morning will come."[2] When the Savior told us to "forgive all men" (Doctrine and Covenants 65:10), we can be certain that admonition includes forgiving ourselves.

> ### *Self-Reflection:*
> *Is there something you cannot forgive yourself for? Now is the time to do it.*

21

I'll Go Where You Want Me to Go

"And it came to pass that the Lord did warn me, that I, Nephi,
should depart from them and flee into the wilderness, and all
those who would go with me." (2 Nephi 5:5)

AFTER LEHI'S DEATH IN THE PREVIOUS CHAPTER, DIVISIONS IN-
creased between Nephi and his brethren. In fact, Nephi "did cry
much unto the Lord . . . because of [their] anger" (2 Nephi 5:1). He
wrote, "But behold their anger did increase against me, insomuch that
they did seek to take away my life" (2 Nephi 5:2). They believed that
Nephi sought to rule over them, and they blamed many of their troubles on him. They assumed that if they killed him, they would "not be
afflicted more because of his words" (2 Nephi 5:3).

Luckily for Nephi, he had the Lord to keep him safe, and He
warned him, saying that Nephi "should depart from them and flee
into the wilderness, and all those who would go with [him]" (2 Nephi
5:5). He took his family "and also Zoram and his family, and Sam . . .
and his family, and Jacob and Joseph, [his] younger brethren, and
also [his] sisters, and all those who would go with [him] who believed
in the warnings and revelations of God" (2 Nephi 5:6). After many

days traveling, they came to a place they decided was a good spot and settled there to build a new city.

Nephi had traveled to an unknown place. All he had was the Lord's direction. He listened and moved forward despite not knowing how it would all work out. When reading this account, especially 2 Nephi 5:5, I thought of the challenges and work of packing up and moving in our day.

Moving is hard and stressful but even more so if you don't know where you're going or why you're going there. This happened to Diony and me soon after we were married. I had only been living in Utah a short time before meeting her, and there were a lot of changes I was adjusting to. Several months after we got married, I began to wonder if the area where we were living was where we were supposed to stay.

One morning as I wrote in my journal, I penned, "I wish to know God's will. I pray to hear. I wonder if we're supposed to move and be somewhere else, and if so, where? Does it matter?"

At that very moment, a clear thought impressed upon me through the Spirit: "Yes, it *does* matter. And there's a specific place He wants you." Twelve days later, I learned through personal revelation where the Lord would have us move—a city 1100 miles away where we had no history, no family, no friends, no employment, and no connections of any kind.

I was reluctant to tell Diony.

When I had previously brought up the idea of us possibly moving, she had not been receptive. Eleven months before, just weeks before I met her, she had moved into a new house, a new ward, and a new neighborhood after much searching, struggling, and contemplating where God wanted *her*. At that time, she knew God had directed her there, and she wasn't expecting or wanting to go through it all again so soon. She also had many close friends, a great nursing job where she had gained seniority, and most importantly, most of her adult children and grandchildren lived nearby. But the next morning on her day off, after spending a little time gathering my thoughts and my courage, I told her what I had felt we were supposed to do.

She was shocked.

The next several days were very challenging as we tried to come to terms with this big, unplanned change in our lives. After lots of discussion, a few tears, and a priesthood blessing, Diony agreed to seek her own answer. It came soon, and it was clearly from the Lord.

Four days later, after a sixteen-hour drive, we arrived in Kansas City, Missouri, with the intention to see what it was like and find out if God's plan would be further revealed. To our astonishment, on that short trip we were led to make an offer to buy a house. It was accepted, and two months later we moved.

"The Lord saw it all coming. He planned for it, step by step, as He has done with other changes. . . . He has raised up and prepared faithful people who choose to do hard things well. He has always been lovingly patient in helping us learn 'line upon line, precept upon precept, here a little and there a little.' He is firm in the timing and the sequence of His intentions, yet He ensures that sacrifice often brings continuing blessings that we did not foresee."[1]

> ### *Self-Reflection:*
> *Has the Lord ever asked you to do something others*
> *would consider crazy? What did you do?*

22

WE ARE THE HOUSE OF ISRAEL

*"And now, the words which I shall read are they which Isaiah
spake concerning all the house of Israel; wherefore, they may
be likened unto you, for ye are of the house of Israel. And there
are many things which have been spoken by Isaiah which may
be likened unto you, because ye are of the house of Israel."*
(2 Nephi 6:5)

AFTER NEPHI AND HIS PEOPLE SETTLED IN THEIR NEW HOME IN THE
wilderness, he called his brothers Jacob and Joseph "that they should
be priests and teachers over . . . the people" (2 Nephi 5:26). At the
beginning of chapter 6, forty years had passed since their family left
Jerusalem, and Jacob is teaching the people. He spoke concerning
"things which are, and which are to come" (2 Nephi 6:4), reading
the words of Isaiah that Nephi counseled him to share. Jacob teaches
them, "Ye are the house of Israel" (2 Nephi 6:5).

As members of The Church of Jesus Christ of Latter-day Saints,
we are also the house of Israel.

> In the Church today, you may hear about Israel in expressions like
> "the gathering of Israel." We sing about the "Redeemer of Israel,"
> the "Hope of Israel," and "Ye Elders of Israel." In these cases, we
> aren't talking or singing only about the ancient kingdom of Israel

or the modern nation called Israel. Rather, we are referring to those who have been gathered from the nations of the world into the Church of Jesus Christ. We are referring to people who persevere with God, who earnestly seek His blessings, and who, through baptism, have become His covenant people.

Your patriarchal blessing declares your connection to one of the tribes of the house of Israel. That's more than an interesting piece of family history information. Being a part of the house of Israel means that you have a covenant relationship with Heavenly Father and Jesus Christ. It means that you, like Abraham, are meant to "be a blessing" to God's children. It means, in the words of Peter, that "ye are a chosen generation, a royal priesthood, an holy nation, a peculiar people; that ye should shew forth the praises of him who hath called you out of darkness into his marvelous light." It means that *you* are one who "perseveres with God" as you honor your covenants with Him.[1]

Further, Elder Patrick Kearon taught the following:

You will remember when President Russell M. Nelson issued the following invitation in general conference. He said: "As you study your scriptures . . . , I encourage you to make a list of all that the Lord has promised He will do for covenant Israel. I think you will be astounded!"

Here are just a few of the powerful and comforting promises our family found. Imagine the Lord speaking these words to you—to you who are surviving—because they are for you:
Fear not.
I know your sorrows, and I have come to deliver you.
I will not leave you.
My name is upon you, and my angels have charge over you.
I will do wonders among you.
Walk with me; learn of me; I will give you rest.
I am in your midst.
You are mine.[2]

As members of Jesus Christ's Church, we are the house of Israel, the covenant people of the Lord. Jacob goes on to teach from the book of Isaiah for the rest of this chapter and the next two chapters (see 2 Nephi 6–8). Later in this book, Nephi instructs and shares the teachings of Isaiah for thirteen more chapters (see 2 Nephi 12–24), which have historically been challenging for many to understand and relate to. But with prayer, study, and earnest effort, these chapters can be incredibly enlightening to the very things that we have, are, and will go through in the world today. As I've studied and read the Book of Mormon this time with a more pure intent to hear Him for myself, I've experienced this personally and my own understanding has increased.

Self-Reflection:
Do you feel like the covenant the Lord made with the house of Israel is active in your life?

23

Deceptions of Satan

"And our spirits must have become like unto him, and we
become devils, angels to a devil, to be shut out from the presence
of our God, and to remain with the father of lies, in misery,
like unto himself; yea, to that being who beguiled our first
parents, who transformeth himself nigh unto an angel of light,
and stirreth up the children of men unto secret combinations
of murder and all manner of secret works of darkness."
(2 Nephi 9:9)

Jacob finished teaching from Isaiah but continued to share the gospel with his people. His teachings are a beautiful testimony of the things that he knows. Speaking of Christ's Atonement, He explains, "Wherefore, it must needs be an infinite Atonement. . . . For behold, if the flesh should rise no more [after mortal death] our spirits must become subject to that angel who fell from before the presence of the Eternal God, and became the devil to rise no more. . . . And we become devils, angels to a devil, to be shut out from the presence of our God" (2 Nephi 9:7–9).

These verses remind us that if it were not for the Atonement and Resurrection of Jesus Christ, we would all become like the devil.

President James E. Faust taught the following:

I think we will witness increasing evidence of Satan's power as the kingdom of God grows stronger. I believe Satan's ever-expanding efforts are some proof of the truthfulness of this work. In the future the opposition will be both more subtle and more open. It will be masked in greater sophistication and cunning, but it will also be more blatant. . . .

Who has not heard and felt the enticings of the devil? His voice often sounds so reasonable and his message so easy to justify. It is an enticing, intriguing voice with dulcet tones. It is neither hard nor discordant. No one would listen to Satan's voice if it sounded harsh or mean. If the devil's voice were unpleasant, it would not entice people to listen to it. . . .

Some of Satan's most appealing lines are "Everyone does it"; "If it doesn't hurt anybody else, it's all right"; "If you feel all right about it, it's OK"; or "It's the 'in' thing to do." These subtle entreaties make Satan the great imitator, the master deceiver, the arch counterfeiter, and the great forger. . . .

The First Presidency described Satan: "He is working under such perfect disguise that many do not recognize either him or his methods. There is no crime he would not commit, no debauchery he would not set up, no plague he would not send, no heart he would not break, no life he would not take, no soul he would not destroy. He comes as a thief in the night; he is a wolf in sheep's clothing." Satan is the world's master in the use of flattery, and he knows the great power of speech. He has always been one of the great forces of the world. . . .

I once heard [a man] say, "The devil is not smart because he is the devil; he is smart because he is old." Indeed, the devil is old, and he was not always the devil. Initially, he was not the perpetrator of evil. He was with the hosts of heaven in the beginning. He was "an angel of God who was in authority in the presence of God."[1]

This scripture tells us that Satan "transformeth himself nigh unto an angel of light" when he "beguiled our first parents" (2 Nephi 9:9), Adam and Eve. I have often thought of having angelic visitors and have even hoped for such visitations. But what if it was Satan in disguise? It comforts me to know that if that was ever to happen to me, we have been given a method in the Doctrine and Covenants to determine the truth:

When a messenger comes saying he has a message from God, offer him your hand and request him to shake hands with you. If he be an angel he will do so, and you will feel his hand. If he be the spirit of a just man made perfect he will come in his glory; for that is the only way he can appear—Ask him to shake hands with you, but he will not move, because it is contrary to the order of heaven for a just man to deceive; but he will still deliver his message. If it be the devil as an angel of light, when you ask him to shake hands he will offer you his hand, and you will not feel anything; you may therefore detect him. (Doctrine and Covenants 129:4–8)

Understanding more of the devils' deceptions, enticements, and methods can help us to learn how to better detect the tools he uses and how to recognize, avoid, and reject him. When his influence is felt, casting him out with any and all of his demons by commanding them to depart in the name of Jesus Christ is a powerful remedy.

While serving my mission in the Canary Islands, my companion and I experienced this one evening while walking toward home down a dark country road. When we approached an unlit building with cinder block walls and no windows, an evil feeling suddenly encompassed us. The air felt noticeably colder, and we were quickly weighed down with anxiety and fear. I told my companion that I felt like there were dark spirits in this place and that we should cast them out. As soon as we did—raising our hands and commanding them to depart in the name of Jesus Christ—we felt immediate relief. As we continued safely on our way, I experienced a strong impression testifying to me this was an example of Jesus Christ's power over Satan.

"Since Satan is the author of all evil in the world, it would therefore be essential to realize that he is the influence behind the opposition to the work of God. Alma stated the issue succinctly: 'For I say unto you that whatsoever is good cometh from God, and whatsoever is evil cometh from the devil' (Alma 5:40)."[2]

Self-Reflection:
What can you do to more readily recognize Satan's deceptions?

24

What Is Good and What Is Evil

"Wo unto them that call evil good, and good evil, that put darkness for light, and light for darkness, that put bitter for sweet, and sweet for bitter!" (2 Nephi 15:20)

Another of Satan's objectives is to convince the world and society that good is evil and evil is good. Nephi shares a total of thirteen chapters in succession of Isaiah's record. In this verse, from those chapters, we continue recognizing more of Satan's lies to the world as he tries to confuse us by distorting truth and labeling "darkness for light, and light for darkness" (2 Nephi 15:20).

In a Brigham Young University devotional, Elder Quentin L. Cook shared the following:

> I had a provocative meeting with an internationally recognized advertising expert a few months ago. We were discussing the influence of evil and the consequences of bad choices.
>
> He envisioned an interesting hypothetical account of Lucifer meeting with an advertising agency. The adversary described his dilemma: he and his followers had rebelled and rejected the Father's plan and had come to understand that they could not prevail

against God. Lucifer understood that while the Father's plan was about joy and happiness, his own plan resulted in grief and misery. The problem, Lucifer explained to the ad executive, was how to attract followers.

It was determined that Lucifer's only hope of success was to achieve a paradigm shift or values inversion—in other words, to characterize the Father's plan as resulting in grief and misery and Lucifer's plan as resulting in joy and happiness.

This hypothetical meeting serves a useful purpose. The truth is, not only do the enemies of the Father's plan attempt to undermine the doctrine and principles of the plan, but they also attempt to mischaracterize the blessings that flow from the plan. Their basic effort is to make that which is good, righteous, and joyful seem miserable.[1]

This values inversion seems to have taken hold in many, if not most, things in today's world. Years ago, in 1965, a famous broadcaster said over the air:

> If I were the devil . . . the Prince of Darkness, I'd want to engulf the whole world in darkness. And I'd have a third of its real estate, and four-fifths of its population, but I wouldn't be happy until I had seized the ripest apple on the tree—Thee. So I'd set about however necessary to take over the United States. I'd subvert the churches first—I'd begin with a campaign of whispers. With the wisdom of a serpent, I would whisper to you as I whispered to Eve: "Do as you please."
>
> To the young, I would whisper that "The Bible is a myth." I would convince them that man created God instead of the other way around. I would confide that what's bad is good, and what's good is "square." And the old, I would teach to pray, after me, "Our Father, which art in Washington . . ."
>
> And then I'd get organized. I'd educate authors in how to make lurid literature exciting, so that anything else would appear dull and uninteresting. I'd threaten TV with dirtier movies and vice versa. I'd pedal narcotics to whom I could. I'd sell alcohol to ladies and gentlemen of distinction. I'd tranquilize the rest with pills.
>
> If I were the devil I'd soon have families that war with themselves, churches at war with themselves, and nations at war with themselves; until each in its turn was consumed. And with

promises of higher ratings I'd have mesmerizing media fanning the flames. If I were the devil I would encourage schools to refine young intellects, but neglect to discipline emotions—just let those run wild, until before you knew it, you'd have to have drug sniffing dogs and metal detectors at every schoolhouse door.

Within a decade I'd have prisons overflowing, I'd have judges promoting pornography—soon I could evict God from the courthouse, then from the schoolhouse, and then from the houses of Congress. And in His own churches I would substitute psychology for religion, and deify science. I would lure priests and pastors into misusing boys and girls and church money. If I were the devil I'd make the symbols of Easter an egg and the symbol of Christmas a bottle.

If I were the devil I'd take from those who have, and give to those who wanted until I had killed the incentive of the ambitious. And what do you bet I couldn't get whole states to promote gambling as the way to get rich? I would caution against extremes and hard work, in Patriotism, in moral conduct. I would convince the young that marriage is old-fashioned, that swinging is more fun, that what you see on TV is the way to be. And thus I could undress you in public, and I could lure you into bed with diseases for which there is no cure.

In other words, if I were the devil I'd just keep right on doing what he's doing.[2]

This was almost sixty years ago! Today it seems the world has adopted even more satanic deceit into common perception, practice, and law. It seems that everywhere I look, I can see Satan's influence and how well he is doing with his paradigm shift.

Self-Reflection:
Where do you see the devil's values inversion affecting your life?

25

"THE FORMULA"

"Wherefore, ye must press forward with a steadfastness in Christ, having a perfect brightness of hope, and a love of God and of all men. Wherefore, if ye shall press forward, feasting upon the word of Christ, and endure to the end, behold, thus saith the Father: Ye shall have eternal life." (2 Nephi 31:20)

IN THIS CHAPTER, NEPHI IS TEACHING AND PROPHESYING ABOUT THE doctrine of Christ, emphasizing the importance of speaking "plainly," for the "Lord God giveth light unto the understanding; for he speaketh to men according to their language" (2 Nephi 31:3). He teaches about the strait and narrow path that leads to eternal life and how the gate to enter it is through repentance and baptism by water—the same way Jesus Christ was baptized. Then he continues testifying of how to gain eternal life—a process that includes certain steps, including endurance.

A brother calls this scripture "the formula" and shared the following experience about it.

He was addicted to pornography from age twenty-three to age forty-seven. He is now fifty-three and has been freed from its hold over him through the Atonement of Jesus Christ and a lot of therapy that Christ led him to.

He loves the Book of Mormon—it speaks of Christ and tells him all things that he should do. He has found answers for his life and witnessed miracles as he's studied its passages. Many references are made to sin and addictions of the flesh, which *we* have agency to choose to overcome through Christ as we "awake from a deep sleep . . . and shake off the awful chains by which [we] are bound" (2 Nephi 1:13). With our agency, we have the power to "not choose eternal death, according to the will of the flesh . . . which giveth the spirit of the devil power to captivate" (2 Nephi 2:29). Porn captivated him—he was so addicted.

Nephi teaches us to "turn away from your sins; shake off the chains from him that would bind you fast; [and] come unto that God who is the rock of your salvation" (2 Nephi 9:45). Nephi, a prophet of God, also openly wrote about himself, "O wretched man that I am! Yea, my heart sorroweth because of my flesh; my soul grieveth because of mine iniquities. I am encompassed about, because of the temptations and the sins which do so easily beset me" (2 Nephi 4:17–18).

We all struggle with sin and temptation. We all need to be strengthened.

Nephi went on to write, "Nevertheless, I know in whom I have trusted. My God hath been my support" (2 Nephi 4:19–20).

Later in the Book of Mormon, Ammon rejoiced and praised God that thousands of their brethren had been "loosed . . . from the chains of hell" (Alma 26:14). Jesus loosed those chains so they could then shake them off. He is the way to overcoming addictions of the flesh. To receive His help, we must first humble ourselves: "And whoso knocketh, to him will he open," (2 Nephi 9:42). Then we must choose Him and His way, for we "are free to choose liberty and eternal life, through the great Mediator . . . or to choose captivity and death" (2 Nephi 2:27).

His Atonement frees us from our sins and our shame.

Nephi teaches us to glory in God's goodness when he writes, "Awake, my soul! No longer droop [have shame] in sin. Rejoice [have gratitude], O my heart, and give place no more for the enemy of my soul" (2 Nephi 4:28). And because of His mercy, we must strive to "remember him, and lay aside our sins, and not hang down our heads, for we are not cast off" (2 Nephi 10:20).

For so many years, as this brother struggled with his addiction, he hung his head down and was ashamed of himself and his past. But as he has heard the Savior's voice through reading and studying the Book of Mormon, he has learned that he doesn't have to feel that way. He is not cast off—he has hope in Him. As he has personally experienced the "awful reality" (2 Nephi 9:47) and consequence of sin, Christ has "awakened him" and changed his heart. He now looks at sin differently and can relate to these words penned by Nephi: "My soul abhorreth sin, and my heart delighteth in righteousness; and I will praise the holy name of my God" (2 Nephi 9:49). His Jesus has redeemed him!

Now back to the formula: As we press forward steadfastly focusing on Jesus Christ, applying His word will give us hope and tell us what we should do. And if we never give up His ways, we will gain eternal life.

Self-Reflection:
To what part of your life can you apply this formula?

PART III

THE BOOK OF JACOB
(ABOUT 544–421 BC)

"As you prayerfully study the Book of Mormon every day, you will make better decisions—every day."

—President Russell M. Nelson[1]

26

Spiritually Defining Memories

"And he gave me, Jacob, a commandment that I should write upon these plates a few of the things which I considered to be most precious. . . . And if there were preaching which was sacred, or revelation which was great, or prophesying, . . . I should engraven [them] upon these plates." (Jacob 1:2, 4)

The book of Jacob begins fifty-five years after Lehi and his family left Jerusalem, with Nephi asking his younger brother, Jacob, to take over the writing on the "small plates" (Jacob 1:1).

As I recently read these scriptures, focusing on the words in Jacob 1:4—*precious, sacred, revelation, great,* and *prophesy*—the Spirit taught me that these are some of the things God wants me to write about in my personal journal as they occur.

The following quote about journal-keeping really spoke to me, further expanding the thoughts and feelings I had while reading in Jacob: "Our journals should become our own personal revelation. If we are careful and diligent in recording the promptings and insights we receive, we will begin to see a pattern of how the Spirit works in our lives. We can be blessed as we write about answers to prayers, scriptural understandings, and our struggles to draw closer to the Lord."[1]

When attending Brigham Young University Education Week in the summer of 2021, one of the speakers in a class Trent and I attended on personal revelation talked about this as well. From my notes, I recall how the teacher said that as we write down spiritual impressions, feelings, and experiences, He will trust us with more such experiences and direction. Recording them in our journal lets Him know we are listening and recognizing Him. Writing promptings and insights we gain makes them clearer, expands our understanding, and may even bring more revelation. And when personal revelation is recorded, we remember it! This helps us draw upon it at later times in our lives when we may be struggling or need extra spiritual strength.

Similar counsel was given at a devotional I attended in Independence, Missouri, in November 2022. Sister Camille N. Johnson, the Relief Society General President, was the highlighted speaker to a large group of Relief Society sisters from multiple stakes. She reminded us to look intentionally for ways Heavenly Father and the Savior show us we are known and loved, often through small and simple ways, and record them in our journal to recall and remember when we are feeling down or low. The fact that I'm hearing this repeatedly from several sources, including my own pondering of the Book of Mormon, lets me know doing this is important!

Writing down the precious and sacred times of hearing Him, in big ways and small, and making a point to recognize that God is aware of us, loves us, and is helping us can increase our peace and remembrance that we *are* His.

Consider this story shared in the *Ensign*:

A young mother, exhausted and discouraged, sat down to write in her journal one night. Instead, she began reading some of the earliest entries. She was amazed by the optimism and enthusiasm with which she had viewed her life five years before. Could that woman really have been her?

As she continued to view life through the journal entries of this energetic young woman . . . she realized that she was reading about herself and that she still possessed the same qualities. . . . She determined to show the same courage again. When she finished reading, she had found renewed confidence in her own strength and ability to endure."[1]

We can understand from studying the scriptures and the history of the Church that keeping records is important to our Heavenly Father and the Lord.

In the Book of Moses, Adam and Eve were taught to keep a "book of remembrance" (Moses 6:5), and in the Book of Mormon, the Lord Himself "commanded that [records] should be written; therefore it was written according as he commanded" (3 Nephi 23:13).

In modern times, instructions were also given to Joseph Smith and other early Church leaders: "Behold, there shall be a record kept among you" (Doctrine and Covenants 21:1), which "shall be for the good of the church, and for the rising generations" (Doctrine and Covenants 69:8).

As we diligently try to record our own personal promptings and revelation in our journals, we have this promise from an apostle: "When personal difficulty, doubt, or discouragement darken our path, or when world conditions beyond our control lead us to wonder about the future, the spiritual defining memories . . . [can be] like luminous stones that help brighten the road ahead, assuring us that God knows us, loves us, and has sent His Son, Jesus Christ, to help us return home."[2]

Self-Reflection:
How often do you write in a journal?

27

Firm Minds

"Look unto God with firmness of mind, and pray unto him with exceeding faith, and he will console you in your afflictions, and he will plead your cause, and send justice upon those who seek your destruction. Feast upon his love, for ye may, if your minds are firm, forever." (Jacob 3:1–2)

Jacob has been speaking at the temple to the people of Nephi (defined as any people who were friendly to Nephi and his posterity and didn't seek their destruction) soon after the death of his older brother Nephi. He used "plainness" (Jacob 2:11), as commanded by the Lord, to those who were lifted up in pride and those who were not living the law of chastity.

Then Jacob addressed those who were pure in heart who were suffering from others' choices and sin. He gave those people some amazing promises that we can also apply to ourselves regarding the importance of looking to God with "firmness of mind" (Jacob 3:1) and the blessings that come from doing so.

I love those blessings listed in Jacob 3:1–2—consolation in affliction, Christ pleading our cause, and us feasting upon His love. The word *feast* comes from the Latin term *festus* relating to being festive or joyous.[1] To me, these promises mean that I can feel His love for me "joyously." When I reflected on these things, I was filled with peace despite my current challenges, and it renewed my hope in my Savior that He would help me through them as I continued to "firmly" focus on Him.

Next, I looked up synonyms for the word *firm*. Ones that especially stood out to me as fitting in the context Jacob used included the following: solid, certain, resolute, unyielding, steady, strong, determined, definite, fixed, and unwavering. All of these gave me a clearer picture and increased my understanding of the message Jacob was sharing.

I found the word *firm* and *firmness* repeated several times throughout the Book of Mormon by other prophets as well. In the book of Alma, Amulek counseled the people to have patience and "bear with those afflictions, with a firm hope that ye shall one day rest from all your afflictions" (Alma 34:41). Helaman recorded that as the "humble" part of the people fasted and prayed often, they "did wax stronger and stronger in their humility, and firmer and firmer in the faith of Christ, unto the filling their souls with joy and consolation . . . because of their yielding their hearts unto God" (Helaman 3:35). And Moroni's counsel on repentance included asking "with a firmness unshaken" to not give in to temptation and to "serve the true and living God" (Mormon 9:28).

In the New Testament, I read that when we are not firm, we become like "a wave of the sea driven with the wind and tossed" (James 1:6), for a "double minded man [or woman] is unstable" (James 1:8). Whether our afflictions come from others' choices, or from the inevitable challenges of living a mortal life in an imperfect world that refine us in "the furnace of affliction" (1 Nephi 20:10), we can still remain steadfast and firm when we turn to Him with trust.

We can know and be certain that "with God, comfort replaces pain, peace replaces turmoil, and hope replaces sorrow. Remaining firm in the faith of Christ will bring His sustaining grace and support. He will convert trial into blessing and, in Isaiah's words, 'give . . . beauty for ashes.'"[2]

A sister was consoled by God in her afflictions with her son, just as Jacob promised can happen, once she learned how to focus her mind more "firmly" on the Savior. She had had a vision of how parenthood would be before she became a mother, but once she started that journey, she was completely caught off guard by the struggle she and her husband faced with one of their children. Through his toddler and preschool years, the situation worsened, and together they did everything they could to counteract the behavioral challenges they had with him. Finally, when he started school and received a diagnosis, they began to get answers. Starting him on recommended medication brought renewed hope, but when his behavior grew worse, her last bit of hope slipped away.

One day, when he was six, facing another one of his many daily tantrums, she wanted to give up. With tears covering her cheeks, she sought solace in her room through prayer. She wondered if Heavenly Father understood how hard things were. She thought, "If He truly loved me, wouldn't He take this burden away?" She thought she understood the nature of trials, but this one kept continuing, and the weight of it was heavy.

The answer she received to that prayer helped her realize she needed to go to the temple to be strengthened, and she needed to stop letting negative thoughts of self-pity fill her mind. She also was guided to receive a priesthood blessing from her husband, and she became more diligent in praying daily for guidance and inspiration on how to help their son. She also learned to quickly pray for help before approaching her son when he was having an emotional meltdown.

The changes she saw and felt were immediate, and her mind was flooded with new ideas and ways to help her son. She learned to rely on God more and more, realizing He knows all things and loved her son even more than she did. She also learned to find happiness in the small moments, even though there were still many hard times.[3]

This sister's trial of emotional affliction, which didn't have a time-limit ending, became easier to bear as she took Jacob's counsel to heart. She kept her mind firmly "feasting upon God's love" by relying and trusting in Him for strength and understanding greater than her own. Her example can help us look differently—with God—at the hard things we can't change in our own lives.

Self-Reflection:
How "firm" is your determination to follow the Lord?

28

THE SPIRIT SPEAKS TRUTH

"For the Spirit speaketh the truth and lieth not. Wherefore, it speaketh of things as they really are, and of things as they really will be; wherefore these things are manifested unto us plainly, for the salvation of our souls." (Jacob 4:13)

IN *DOCTRINES OF SALVATION*, WE CAN LEARN MANY THINGS ABOUT THE Holy Ghost. He is "the third member of the Godhead. He is a Spirit, in the form of a man."[1] The Holy Ghost has many roles, including "Comforter, Testator, Revelator, Sanctifier, Holy Spirit, Holy Spirit of Promise, the Spirit of Truth, Spirit of the Lord, and Messenger of the Father and the Son."[2]

In this chapter, Jacob teaches about the mission of the Holy Ghost and how He testifies of truth. Later on in the Book of Mormon, Moroni teaches that "by the power of the Holy Ghost, ye may know the truth of all things" (Moroni 10:5).

I have felt the Holy Ghost testify of truth repeatedly in my own life as I've searched for answers to understand my purpose, to know God's will for me, to know how to better fulfill my varied roles, and to gain knowledge about things I'm seeking to grasp and comprehend. His voice is not loud but can feel piercing and calmly clear—different from other voices or my own thoughts.

"As we study, ponder, and pray about gospel truths, the Holy Ghost enlightens our minds and quickens our understanding. He causes the truth to be indelibly written in our souls and can cause a mighty change to occur in our hearts."[3]

Modern-day prophets have taught, "The Spirit of God speaking to the spirit of man has power to impart the truth with greater effect and understanding than the truth can be imparted by personal contact even with heavenly beings. Through the Holy Ghost the truth is woven into the very fibre and sinews of the body so that it cannot be forgotten."[4]

Elder Matthew L. Carpenter said:

In my own life, I have found that as I read the Book of Mormon, I regularly feel the Holy Ghost witnessing of the truth of what I read. And then I receive additional blessings. Because I feel the Holy Ghost witness of the truth of the words in the Book of Mormon, while he is witnessing of these truths, my heart and mind are also open to receiving other impressions about what I should do in other aspects of my life. The Holy Ghost truly guides me in truth, and teaches me all things, as the scriptures promise. I have received guidance in work matters and in family matters. I have received direction in Church callings and help in solving other problems I am facing. . . . If I listen and seek, I often receive additional guidance in what I should do in other aspects of my life.[5]

> ### Self-Reflection:
> *How have you felt the Holy Ghost witness truth to you as you've read the Book of Mormon?*

29

I Could Not Be Shaken

"And he had hope to shake me from the faith . . . for I truly had seen angels, and they had ministered unto me. And also, I had heard the voice of the Lord speaking unto me . . . wherefore, I could not be shaken." (Jacob 7:5)

I love Jacob's faithfulness in this last chapter of his book when he defends the existence of Jesus Christ and His doctrine against a man named Sherem. This man diligently labored to deceive the hearts of the people of Nephi by flattering them with his speech and perfect knowledge of their language. But with help from above, Jacob absolutely held his own during their dialogue and interaction. As he described in Jacob 7:5, "I could not be shaken." The power of the Lord was definitely with him.

Jacob wrote, "I had requested it of my Father who was in heaven; for he had heard my cry and answered my prayer. And it came to pass that peace and the love of God was restored again among the people" (Jacob 7:22–23).

There are times in our own lives when our faith is questioned by others, and when it is, we can solicit help from above. Angels beyond the veil can come to our aid in many earthly circumstances we may face, and we can receive direction and comfort from the Spirit of the Lord.

I experienced this "questioning" from someone I was very close to. His doubts and fears shook me because of the place he held in my life. As our conversations increased in frequency and intensity, I finally told him I couldn't continue to discuss his spiritual struggles, which included the topic of early Church history. The weight of his doubts was beginning to weigh heavily on me, and each succeeding conversation felt void of the Spirit and seemed to invite darkness. I encouraged him to pray for help, and in looking for peace and direction, I went to my knees and did the same.

I received comfort from hands unseen and was reassured to hold on to the spiritual truths that had guided my life. I was also directed by the Spirit to attend the temple for further support and answers.

I did.

While I was there attending an endowment session, I received a clear response to one of the more significant issues the person close to me had been pushing that had created inner turmoil. My heart was immediately lightened as I felt truth reconfirmed. Once again, I felt I was on solid ground, and this time, my foundation was stronger.

Elder Neil L. Andersen said, "How do you remain 'steadfast and immovable' during a trial of faith? You immerse yourselves in the very things that helped build your core of faith: you exercise faith in Christ, you pray, you ponder the scriptures, you repent, you keep the commandments, and you serve others. Whatever you do, don't step away from the Church! Distancing yourself from the kingdom of God during a trial of faith is like leaving the safety of a secure storm cellar just as the tornado comes into view."[1]

Perhaps the most important key of all is this: "When we are firm in keeping our covenants and living true to the light we have, the Lord will bless our lives and give us inspiration. . . . These tender mercies . . . are very personal, direct experiences between us and our Heavenly Father. They are light and knowledge. No amount of reading or studying third-hand experiences can match the power of first-hand experiences given to us by the mercy and love of our Father."[2]

Self-Reflection:
Are you remembering to "doubt your doubts before you doubt your faith"? [3]

PART IV

THE BOOK OF ENOS
(ABOUT 544–421 BC)

"As you ponder what you study [in the Book of Mormon], the windows of heaven will open, and you will receive answers to your own questions and direction for your own life."

—President Russell M. Nelson[1]

30

Don't Look Backward

*"And I, Enos, knew that God could not lie; wherefore my guilt
was swept away." (Enos 1:6)*

At this point, Enos has taken over the writings for his father, Jacob. Before Jacob died, he told Enos the things Nephi had commanded him concerning the record, and Enos agreed to continue keeping the record in obedience to those commands. He begins the only chapter of his book by talking about the things his father had taught him and how his soul "hungered" (Enos 1:4) to know God better.

Enos recorded the "wrestle which [he] had before God, before [he] received a remission of his sins" (Enos 1:2.4), crying out in mighty prayer and supplication for his own soul. "And there came a voice unto [him] saying: Enos, thy sins are forgiven thee, and thou shalt be blessed" (Enos 1:5). In the next verse, he writes, "Wherefore my guilt was swept away" (Enos 1:6). The Lord explained that it had happened because of his faith in Christ and told him, "Thy faith hath made thee whole" (Enos 1:8).

Elder Dale G. Renlund taught, "When we sincerely repent, no spiritual scar remains, no matter what we have done, how serious it was, or how many times we repeated it. As often as we repent and seek forgiveness with real intent, we can be forgiven."[1]

Sometimes, forgiving ourselves is tough!

An eighteen-year-old woman wrestled with this. She started taking lessons with the missionaries, and some of the things she learned about living a life that reflected the teachings of Christ crushed her. She had not been following the law of chastity, and she wondered if she was broken and too far gone. She worried she would never be fully forgiven, even if she repented. She was filled with thoughts of how she had let Christ down without even knowing it, and she considered that following the law of chastity was not attainable for her.

The adversary flooded her mind with questions, causing her to second-guess the things the missionaries were teaching her. She was also in a relationship at that time that didn't make staying morally clean a priority. She wondered if The Church of Jesus Christ of Latter-day Saints was for her, but she couldn't deny the truths she was feeling within it or that Joseph Smith was a prophet. This knowledge helped her realize that the law of chastity must also be a true commandment of the Lord.

It was time to look forward, not backward. She accepted the challenge to apply the law of chastity to her life.

There were instances she fell short as she struggled to break the cycle of her past. When she finally made it to the point where she was obeying the law of chastity, she still kept remembering all the moments she had messed up. Since then, she has said, "I have realized that the Lord will forgive us, but we must learn to forgive ourselves as well. Heavenly Father wants us to recognize our mistakes, repent, strive to do better, and move on. Satan, however, wants us to be chained to our sins. Those feelings of failure were Satan telling me, 'You can't do this. You're crazy for even thinking you can.'"[2]

As time has passed since she joined the Church, she has had blessings come from following the law of chastity. She doesn't feel broken and confused anymore. She has recognized and felt the Lord's love for her and the strength that comes from Christ's Atonement.

Dwelling on our mistakes, instead of learning and growing from them, holds us in the past and keeps us from moving forward. Like Enos, we can experience and choose faith in God's promises, knowing

"God doesn't lie." When we truly repent and are forgiven, we don't have to look backward and dwell on our mistakes, pain, suffering, or guilt. That torment can be "swept away" because of Jesus Christ's atoning sacrifice, and we can experience joy and peace.

> ### Self-Reflection:
> *Are you looking forward or backward?*

PART V

THE BOOK OF JAROM
(ABOUT 420–361 BC)

"As you daily immerse yourself in the Book of Mormon, you can be immunized against the evils of the day, even the gripping plague of pornography and other mind-numbing addictions."

—President Russell M. Nelson[1]

31

A PRICKED HEART

"Wherefore, the prophets, and the priests, and the teachers, did labor diligently, exhorting with all long-suffering the people to diligence. . . . And it came to pass that by so doing . . . they did prick their hearts with the word, continually stirring them up unto repentance." (Jarom 1:11–12)

AT THE BEGINNING OF THE BOOK OF JAROM, 179 YEARS HAD PASSED since Lehi left Jerusalem, and Enos has passed the plates on to his son Jarom to continue their genealogy. Jarom mentions that the plates are small and says, "What could I write more than my fathers have written? For have they not revealed the plan of salvation?" (Jarom 1:2). He felt that was sufficient, but he did go on and write thirteen more verses before he passed the plates on to his son Omni fifty-nine years later.

Some of the people had hard hearts, and others were faithful and received revelations and direction from the Holy Spirit. The people continued to multiply and spread on the land, some even becoming quite prosperous. Jarom recorded the diligence with which the leaders taught the importance of following the commandments of God, pricking the people's hearts with His words, "continually stirring them up unto repentance" (Jarom 1:12).

Definitions of the verb *prick* that I found applicable in this scripture context were "to pierce slightly with a sharp point"; "to affect with anguish, grief, or remorse"; "to guide or urge"; "to mark or distinguish".[1]

When our hearts are "pricked" or we feel a piercing, we can use that attention-getting sensation to become more humble and aware of something in our life that needs our attention—maybe something we need to do, stop doing, change, fix, improve, or repent of.

When I consistently put myself in places I can more easily feel God—like attending church and the temple, engaging in activities that invite His Spirit, and studying the scriptures and general conference talks—I more readily recognize and receive the sensation of "pricking." These experiences help me know when I need to redirect and alter things in my life to keep focused on the covenant path.

I recorded in my journal an experience I had with a fellow ward member that upset me. I didn't like how something was being handled, and I felt that the person involved was not keeping their word after committing they would do something relating to a Church calling. The situation felt messy and unorganized—the opposite of how I work best. Because I didn't know the person very well, I wasn't sure how to fix the problem or how to let go of my increasing frustration.

I prayed for help.

My heart was "pricked" that I needed to be patient and share my feelings kindly but firmly with the other person, offering suggestions of a solution.

I did.

The response I got back from the other person was receptive and positive, and together we were able to address, plan, and organize upcoming activities related to the fulfilling of the calling. I learned that listening to the Spirit and meeting others where they are is vital. I repented of my initial unkind thoughts and feelings and was grateful for the reminder that handling things the Lord's way is always best.

I also draw strength when my heart is "pricked" by words of comfort and counsel that come exactly when I need to hear them. This kind of experience happened to Ezra Thayer during a Sunday sermon given by Hyrum Smith in October 1830. It led to Ezra's conversion, and he later recalled, "Every word touched me to the inmost soul. I thought every word was pointed to me."[2]

Whenever this happens to me, my testimony is strengthened and I am reminded that He knows exactly what I am facing and is sending help.

Self-Reflection:
Can you recognize times in your own life when the Spirit has "pricked" your heart?

PART VI

THE BOOK OF OMNI
(ABOUT 361–130 BC)

"Regardless of how many times you previously may have read the Book of Mormon, there will come into your lives and into your homes an added measure of the Spirit of the Lord."

—President Gordon B. Hinckley[1]

32

ALL GOOD THINGS COME FROM GOD

"[I exhort] all men to come unto God . . . and believe . . . in all things which are good; for there is nothing which is good save it comes from the Lord: and that which is evil cometh from the devil." (Omni 1:25)

THE BOOK OF OMNI, A TOTAL OF ONE CHAPTER, HAS FIVE DIFFERENT authors and covers 231 years in thirty verses. It starts with Omni, who was the son of Jarom. Omni passed the plates to his son Amaron, and Amaron passed them to his brother Chemish. Chemish passed them on to his son Abinadom, and Abinadom gave them to his son Amaleki. Amaleki wrote the most, starting in verse 12 until the end of the chapter. Overall, their writings seemed to indicate that this time frame involved a lengthy period of apostasy and wickedness. In fact, during the last half of the chapter, Amaleki wrote that Mosiah was warned by the Lord to "flee out of the land of Nephi" (Omni 1:12), taking with him as many as would listen.

Eventually, the Lord led them through the wilderness into the land of Zarahemla (in about 200 BC). The people they met there rejoiced because they came with the brass plates, which contained a record of the Jews. Both groups united together, and Mosiah became the king. Amaleki was born during the days of Mosiah and "lived to see his death; and Benjamin, his son, [reigned] in his stead" (Omni 1:23).

Before Amaleki ended his writing and passed the plates on to King Benjamin (because he had no children), he bore his testimony of Jesus Christ, "exhorting all men" to believe in prophesying, revelations, the ministering of angels, the gift of tongues, and "all things which are good" (Omni 1:25).

As I read this verse, I was reminded of all the "good things" in my life, which *all* come from God—simple things, like a warm summer breeze caressing my face, the fragrance of a blooming rose in my garden, brilliant hues of a fiery sunset, the sound of laughter, or a love-filled look from the one dearest to me. To me, all of these are a reflection of *His* love and goodness.

His goodness also goes deeper in my overwhelming gratitude for the Lord's atoning sacrifice for me—for the times He's given me light and compassion when I've wrestled with darkness and despair, and when He's walked beside me through unknown paths until I discern the direction He wants me to go. His plan and His timing is always better than mine.

Do you remember the parable about laborers in the vineyard? It's about a man, a "householder," who hired laborers early in the morning to work for him in his vineyard for an agreed-upon wage. Three hours later he hired more, and after six hours and nine hours, he did the same. Then, at the eleventh hour, he hired more. At the end of the day, he paid them all the same wage, even though they had worked for him different lengths of time. Those who had worked the entire day complained that it was unfair, but the vineyard owner replied, "Friend, I do thee no wrong. . . . Is it not lawful for me to do what I will with my own?" (Matthew 20:13, 15).

This parable is another example of God's goodness. He meets us wherever we are, whenever we are ready to come to Him, and generously offers His help, compassion, and grace equally. He doesn't care if we come early or late—His arms are always outstretched.

When I hear and sing the following words from my favorite hymn, my heart always catches and swells with emotional awe over the sacrifice the Savior made for me:

> And when I think that God, His Son not sparing,
> Sent Him to die, I scarce can take it in;
> That on the cross, my burden gladly bearing,
> He bled and died to take away my sin;
> Then sings my soul, my Savior God to Thee;
> How great Thou art, how great Thou art!"[1]

Self-Reflection:
How have you seen God's goodness in your life?

PART VII

THE WORDS OF MORMON
(ABOUT AD 385)

"The central purpose of the Book of Mormon is its testament of Jesus Christ. Of more than 6,000 verses in the Book of Mormon, far more than half refer directly to Him."

—President Boyd K. Packer[1]

33

FOR A WISE PURPOSE

*"I do this for a wise purpose; for thus it whispereth me,
according to the workings of the Spirit of the Lord. . . . I do not
know all things; but the Lord knoweth all things which are to
come; wherefore, he worketh in me to do according to his will."
(Words of Mormon 1:7)*

THIS BOOK IS WRITTEN BY MORMON. HE WAS A NEPHITE GENERAL, the father of Moroni, a prophet, a record keeper, and the man who compiled and abridged most of the Book of Mormon. It was written several hundred years after Christ came, after Mormon "witnessed almost all the destruction of [his] people" (Words of Mormon 1:1).

It is a bridge between the small plates of Nephi (1 Nephi–Omni) and Mormon's abridgment of the large plates of Nephi (Mosiah–4 Nephi). The small plates didn't include the early reign of King Benjamin, "of whom Amaleki spake" (Words of Mormon 1:3), so Mormon includes a small account of him in this book, the Words of Mormon, to connect to the rest of the Book of Mormon. The Lord inspired Mormon to do this "for a wise purpose" (Words of Mormon 1:7).

If we look back to Nephi's words in 1 Nephi, when he was directed to create two sets of plates (the small and large plates of Nephi), he wrote, "The Lord commanded me to make these plates for a wise purpose in him, which purpose I know not" (1 Nephi 9:5).

Both these prophets, who lived centuries apart, were obedient, trusting in what the Lord asked of them regarding keeping the records, even if they didn't understand exactly why. We know today what God had planned because of what occurred in 1828. Martin Harris lost 116 pages of the manuscript that Joseph Smith translated, which were part of Mormon's abridgment of Nephi's large plates. Joseph Smith was commanded by the Lord not to re-translate those pages because words could be changed to try to discredit him.[1]

Because God had known what would happen, the small plates Nephi had written covered the same history that had been lost. And Mormon used his writing in this book, comprised of 18 verses, to connect the two sets of plates together.

This is a perfect example of using faith to trust that "the Lord knoweth all things," and as we seek to hear His voice, He will guide us to know and do His will.

Self-Reflection:
Have you ever received a prompting to do something you initially didn't understand but later made sense?

PART VIII

THE BOOK OF MOSIAH
(ABOUT 130–92 BC)

"The Book of Mormon acts as a confirming, clarifying, unifying witness of the doctrines taught in the Bible so that there is only 'one Lord, one faith, one baptism.'"

—Elder Tad R. Callister[1]

34

SEARCH THEM DILIGENTLY

"And now, my sons, I would that ye should remember to search them diligently, that ye may profit thereby; and I would that ye should keep the commandments of God, that ye may prosper in the land according to the promises which the Lord made unto our fathers." (Mosiah 1:7)

THE BOOK OF MOSIAH BEGINS WITH AN ACCOUNT OF THE CURRENT king of Zarahemla—King Benjamin, the son of Mosiah. He was the king that Amaleki gave the records to before his death, knowing he was "a just man before the Lord" (Omni 1:25). Many years into King Benjamin's reign, and after many deadly battles with the Lamanites where the king fought by the side of his people with the sword of Laban, there was finally peace in the land (see Words of Mormon 1:12–13, 18).

In this time of peace, and as King Benjamin was aging, he taught his children—Mosiah, Heloram, and Helaman—"in all the language of his fathers" (Mosiah 1:2). He also admonished them to "remember that these sayings are true, and also that these records [which he had received from Amaleki] are true" (Mosiah 1:6). And he told them, "Ye should remember to search them diligently, that ye may profit thereby" (Mosiah 1:7) and keep the commandments that they would prosper according to the promises of the Lord.

I love the phrase "to search them diligently."

All of my life as a member of The Church of Jesus Christ of Latter-day Saints, I have been told to read the scriptures—a constant reminder in almost every class and church meeting from the time I was very young. It got to the point where those words barely registered—it was just on constant repeat and felt like background noise. I did go through times when I read consistently, but mostly it was out of obligation to complete a seminary class or because of a frequently renewed goal to read daily, which only lasted several months at best. While serving on my mission, I studied them every day (a mission rule) and started to see the benefit of doing so—I felt the Spirit with me more. But honestly, it's only been the last ten years of my life, after going through some big personal changes and spiritual commitments I made because of them, that I have learned to more fully "search them diligently."

In a general conference talk, Bishop Dean M. Davies stated:

> Searching the scriptures on a daily basis will also fortify our faith and character. Just as we need food to nourish our physical bodies, our spirits and souls will be replenished and strengthened by feasting upon the words of Christ as contained in the writings of the prophets. Nephi taught, "Feast upon the words of Christ; for behold, the words of Christ will tell you all things what ye should do" (2 Nephi 32:3).
>
> While reading the scriptures is good, reading by itself is insufficient to capture the full breadth and depth of the Savior's teachings. Searching, pondering, and applying the words of Christ as taught in the scriptures will bring wisdom and knowledge beyond our mortal understanding. This will strengthen our commitment and provide the spiritual reserves to do our best in all situations.[1]

Every morning as I study the scriptures, often with Diony, sometimes I only get through one or two verses. Other times, I read several chapters to comprehend the bigger picture at play. Doing this while studying other Church doctrines, along with earnestly praying and writing in my journal on a daily basis, has changed my life. I still have many trials, problems, and challenges, but doing this every single day has strengthened my commitment to follow God in everything, and it's given me spiritual reserves to strive to do my best in all situations.

Self-Reflection:
What does searching the scriptures look like to you?

35

Is Not Far Distant

"For behold, the time cometh, and is not far distant, that with power, the Lord Omnipotent who reigneth, who was, and is from all eternity to all eternity, shall come down from heaven among the children of men, and shall dwell in a tabernacle of clay, and shall go forth amongst men, working mighty miracles, such as healing the sick, raising the dead, causing the lame to walk, the blind to receive their sight, and the deaf to hear, and curing all manner of diseases." (Mosiah 3:5)

After King Benjamin finished talking to his sons, he decided to confer the kingdom on his son Mosiah. He asked his son to make a proclamation throughout the land and gather all the people the next day for that announcement and to impart further counsel to them (see Mosiah 1:9–10). This powerful discourse has become known as King Benjamin's sermon. I like to think of it as my first favorite conference talk—a whole book could be written on his address alone.

Partway through his sermon, he told his people that an angel of the Lord appeared to him in the night and said, "Awake, and hear the words which I shall tell thee; for behold, I am come to declare unto you the glad tidings of great joy" (Mosiah 3:3). This angel then gave him a message to declare to his people, saying, "The time cometh, and is not far distant, that with power, the Lord . . . shall come down from heaven" (Mosiah 3:5).

After reading this, I asked myself, "What was the Lord's timing?" The angel said that the time is coming and not far distant, yet it was still about 123 years from occurring (see 3 Nephi 1:19–21). If I would have been there in the multitude listening to King Benjamin's address, I would have thought that it was going to come *soon*, like at least in my lifetime. However, I would have been wrong.

Let's consider the Second Coming of Christ. In Doctrine and Covenants 34:7, which was received in 1830—192 years ago—it says, "For behold, verily, verily, I say unto you, the time is soon at hand that I shall come in a cloud with power and great glory." Are "soon at hand" and "not far distant" about the same amount of time to the Lord? I think they probably are, but I would have been wrong before, so I may be wrong now. What I do know is that the Lord's timing is *His*, and my duty is just to be ready, always remembering Christ that "his Spirit" (Moroni 4:3) will be with me.

When I want answers *now*, I need to remember that the Lord has His own timing. As Elder Ulisses Soares said:

> We must remember that taking our cross upon ourselves includes being humble and trusting in God and in His infinite wisdom. We must acknowledge that He is aware of each of us and of our needs. It is also necessary to accept the fact that the Lord's timing is different than ours. Sometimes we seek for a blessing and set a time limit for the Lord to fulfill it. We cannot condition our faithfulness to Him by imposing upon Him a deadline for the answers to our desires. When we do this, we resemble the skeptical Nephites from ancient times, who mocked their brothers and sisters by saying that the time was past for the fulfillment of the words spoken by Samuel the Lamanite, creating confusion among those who believed. We need to trust the Lord enough to be still and know that He is God, that He knows all things, and that He is aware of each of us.[1]

With regard to the Second Coming of the Lord, I can also learn from President Nelson, who said: "As I have stated before, the gathering of Israel is the most important work taking place on earth today. One crucial element of this gathering is preparing a people who are able, ready, and worthy to receive the Lord when He comes again, a people who have already chosen Jesus Christ over this fallen world, a people who rejoice in their agency to live the higher, holier laws of Jesus Christ. I call upon you, my dear brothers and sisters, to become this righteous people."[2]

Whether it is "not far distant" or "soon at hand," the key is to have already chosen the Lord and live His law. As President Nelson taught, we must "cherish and honor [our] covenants above all other commitments."[2] As we do so, we can truly become a people ready to receive the Lord, as our prophet has counseled us to do.

Self-Reflection:
How soon is "not far distant" to you, and are you ready?

36

WILLING TO SUBMIT

"For the natural man is an enemy to God, and has been from the fall of Adam, and will be, forever and ever, unless he yields to the enticings of the Holy Spirit, and putteth off the natural man and becometh a saint through the Atonement of Christ the Lord, and becometh as a child, submissive, meek, humble, patient, full of love, willing to submit to all things which the Lord seeth fit to inflict upon him, even as a child doth submit to his father." (Mosiah 3:19)

KING BENJAMIN CONTINUES HIS ADDRESS WITH THE WORDS FROM the angel, testifying of the life of Jesus Christ, including His birth, Atonement, death, and Resurrection (see Mosiah 3:8–11). He then instructs his people and us with this inspiring scripture in Mosiah 3:19.

In order to become more like God and be changed from a natural state to a spiritual one, we need to diligently work on being humble, submissive, and patient in our relationships with others. Little differences can easily grow into big ones if we aren't careful, and when pride gets in the way of love and kindness, the effects can damage relationships and hurt people.

This happened when a family gathered to study the scriptures one morning. The father noticed that some of the family members didn't look excited to participate, and after prayer when they started to read, he saw that one of his daughters didn't have her scriptures with her. He asked her to go to her room and bring back her scriptures. She left unenthusiastically, and after some time passed, she returned. When she sat down, she said, "Do we really have to do this now?"

The father, trying to stay calm, said, "Yes, we have to do this now because this is what the Lord wants us to do."

His daughter protested, "I really don't want to do this now!"

The father lost his patience, raised his voice, and said, "This is *my* home, and we will always read the scriptures in my home!"

The daughter then left the family circle, ran to her room, and slammed the door.

The father knew he had handled the situation poorly and in anger, so he went to his own bedroom and prayed. He asked the Lord for help, knowing he had hurt his daughter. He asked that love and harmony could return to their home. During his prayer, he felt he needed to go and apologize to his daughter.

Outside her closed bedroom door, he stood and gently knocked. She didn't answer. When he slowly opened the door, he saw his daughter crying on her bed. He knelt next to her and in a soft voice told her he was sorry and that he loved her. She stopped crying, and after a minute, she opened her nearby scriptures. After searching briefly, she began to read in Mosiah, "For the natural man is an enemy to God . . . unless he yields to the enticings of the Holy Spirit, and putteth off the natural man and becometh a saint through the Atonement of Christ the Lord, and becometh as a child, submissive, meek, humble, patient, full of love, willing to submit to all things which the Lord seeth fit to inflict upon him, even as a child doth submit to his father" (Mosiah 3:19).

The father thought the scripture had been written for him and that his daughter was teaching him a lesson, but she turned her eyes to him and said, "I'm sorry. I'm sorry."[1]

Both father and daughter learned a lesson that day hearing the Savior's voice in the Book of Mormon through the Holy Ghost.

Putting off the natural man is also the way to overcome the world, which we are instructed to do in Doctrine and Covenants 64:2. As President Nelson taught, "How, then, do we overcome the world?

King Benjamin taught us how. He said that 'the natural man is an enemy to God' and remains so forever '*unless* he yields to the enticings of the Holy Spirit, and putteth off the natural man and becometh a saint through the atonement of Christ the Lord.' Each time you seek for and follow the promptings of the Spirit, each time you do anything good—things that 'the natural man' would not do—you are overcoming the world."[2]

Self-Reflection:

Is there something you are dealing with in a relationship that you can try to overcome by being more humble and patient?

37

Born of Him

*"And now, because of the covenant which ye have made ye shall
be called the children of Christ, his sons, and his daughters; for
behold, this day he hath spiritually begotten you; for ye say that
your hearts are changed through faith on his name; therefore, ye
are born of him and have become his sons and his daughters."*
(Mosiah 5:7)

After King Benjamin finished his address, he desired to know
if his people believed the teachings of the angel and the things that he
had taught and testified to them. "And they all cried with one voice,
saying: Yea, we believe all the words which thou hast spoken unto us;
and also, we know of their surety and truth, because of the Spirit . . .
which has wrought a mighty change in us, or in our hearts" (Mosiah
5:2). Not only did they believe him, but they wanted to enter into a
covenant with God. This was King Benjamin's desire for his people,
and I imagine it brought him great joy.

Because of this covenant, they would be called the "children of
Christ" (Mosiah 5:7), spiritually reborn of God. Through faith, their
hearts were changed and they became His sons and daughters.

What does it mean to be spiritually reborn? One *Ensign* article
explained it this way:

Spiritual rebirth begins and ends with belief in Christ. When repentant souls turn to Christ and seek a new life with him, the processes of rebirth commence. When their belief in the Lord increases until they are able to do the works that he does, "and greater works than these" (John 14:12), their rebirth is perfect, and they are prepared for salvation with him.

The essence of being spiritually reborn is in following the enticings of the Spirit, which "giveth light to every man that cometh into the world . . . [and] hearkeneth to the voice of the Spirit. And every one that hearkeneth to the voice of the Spirit cometh unto God, even the Father" (Doctrine and Covenants 84:46–47). As we obey the promptings of the Spirit, we receive the light and truth necessary for greater degrees of spiritual rebirth. "He that receiveth light, and continueth in God, receiveth more light; and that light groweth brighter and brighter until the perfect day" (Doctrine and Covenants 50:24).[1]

Further, Elder Holland taught the following:

We learn that when repentance is complete, we are born again and leave behind forever the self we once were. To me, none of the many approaches to teaching repentance falls more short than the well-intentioned suggestion that "although a nail may be removed from a wooden post, there will forever be a hole in that post."

We know that repentance (the removal of that nail, if you will) can be a very long and painful and difficult task. . . .

But where repentance is possible, and its requirements are faithfully pursued and completed, there is no "hole left in the post" for the bold reason that it is no longer the same post. It is a new post. We can start again, utterly clean, with a new will and a new way of life.

Through repentance we are changed to what Alma calls "new creatures" (Mosiah 27:26). We are "born again; yea, born of God, changed from [our] carnal and fallen state, to a state of righteousness, being redeemed of God, becoming his sons and daughters" (Mosiah 27:25; see also Mosiah 5:1–12).[2]

To have no holes in that post is a beautiful metaphor, for it is a new post because you have been reborn. When you experience a spiritual rebirth, you become His child and have a new will and way of life.

Self-Reflection:
Do you feel like you have been spiritually reborn? Can you still see that hole in your post?

38

SEER

"But a seer can know of things which are past, and also of things which are to come, and by them shall all things be revealed, or, rather, shall secret things be made manifest, and hidden things shall come to light, and things which are not known shall be made known by them, and also things shall be made known by them which otherwise could not be known." (Mosiah 8:17)

THREE YEARS AFTER HIS ADDRESS, KING BENJAMIN DIED AND MOSIAH began reigning as a righteous king, following his father's counsel (see Mosiah 6:3, 5). At one point, Mosiah wondered what had happened to a group of people that left Zarahemla years earlier, led by a man named Zeniff, to try to claim the land of their inheritance, so he sent a group of sixteen men to try to find out. After forty days of looking, they came to the land where Zeniff had settled. There they found King Limhi, who was Zeniff's grandson (see Mosiah 7:1–9).

After eventual introductions and explanations, these men from Zarahemla, led by Ammon, learned of a set of records from a people that had been as numerous as the hosts of Israel but then were destroyed from off the face of the earth. These records had been found by Limhi's people in their search for Zarahemla years earlier. Limhi was desirous to have the records translated because they were in a foreign language. Ammon informed King Limhi that King Mosiah of Zarahemla was a seer and that he had the ability to translate with a set of stones by the power of God. This made Limhi very happy (see Mosiah 7:10–33).

Just as King Mosiah was a seer, we have seers today. We learn much about what a seer is from Ammon's words in Mosiah 8. He teaches that through a seer, "things shall be made known by them which otherwise could not be known" (Mosiah 8:17).

More can be learned about this topic from an October 2000 general conference address:

> The fundamental responsibility of prophets, seers, and revelators, all of whom bear apostolic authority, is to bear certain testimony of the name of Jesus Christ in all the world. This basic call to be a special witness of His name has remained constant whenever Apostles have been on the earth. This testimony, borne of the Holy Ghost through revelation, was the heart of the New Testament Church and is the heart of the Church today. . . .
>
> Secondly, prophets, seers, and revelators teach the word of God in clarity that all His children may benefit and be blessed through obedience to their teachings. . . .
>
> Thirdly, we sustain 15 men not only as prophets and revelators but as seers also. The presence of seers among us is not much spoken of, yet the ability to see beyond the present lends power and authority to apostolic testimony and teaching. . . .
>
> In the Pearl of Great Price, we read that the Lord instructed Enoch to anoint his eyes with clay, and wash them, that he could see. Enoch did so. "And he beheld . . . things which were not visible to the natural eye; and from thenceforth came the saying abroad in the land: A seer hath the Lord raised up unto his people" (Moses 6:36).
>
> To the question of what our modern seers are making known that otherwise could not be known and what they are seeing that is not visible to the natural eye, I make a very simple response. Listen, ponder, and prayerfully consider what they are teaching and what they are doing. As you do so, a pattern emerges that reveals much, and therein will the answer to this question be found.[1]

Self-Reflection:

What do the fifteen seers on earth today know that you do not? What pattern can you see from these seers' teachings and actions that will reveal much to you?

39

PERCEPTION VERSUS REALITY

"They were a wild, and ferocious, and a blood-thirsty people,
believing in the tradition of their fathers, which is this—
Believing that they were driven out of the land of Jerusalem
because of the iniquities of their fathers, and that they were
wronged in the wilderness by their brethren, and they were also
wronged while crossing the sea." (Mosiah 10:12)

CHAPTERS 9–22 IN MOSIAH TAKE US BACKWARD IN TIME TO THE
record of Zeniff when he led a group of people away from Zarahemla
to seek the lands of his ancestry. They found the Lamanites there in
the land where they wished to live. Zeniff met with the king of the
Lamanites, who allowed them to live in a part of this land. However,
this king had an ulterior motive that when Zeniff's people got estab-
lished in the land and were successful with their flocks and crops, he
would go to war with them to bring them into bondage to support
himself and the Lamanite people (see Mosiah 9:1–10).

Twelve years later, Zeniff fought him off with his armies and
won the battle, after which they lived in peace for twenty-two more
years until the Lamanite king died. This king's son and successor
then decided to go to war again with Zeniff and his people. Zeniff
describes the Lamanites' state of being, saying that they were wild,

bloodthirsty, and believed the traditions of their fathers (see Mosiah 9:11–19; 10:1–12).

As I read Mosiah 10:12, I thought to myself, "What are the 'traditions' that we believe in our society that are actually false?" What traditions do we have the wrong perception about—Satan's perspective? I know that a person's perception is their reality until proven otherwise. In the Lamanites' case, their perception was not based in truth—it was based in lies that were passed down for generations. Satan, being the father of lies, wanted this wild, ferocious, bloodthirsty people to believe those lies.

On the other hand, God, Jesus Christ, and the Holy Ghost only testify of truth. As Elder Renlund taught:

> The Spirit plays a pivotal role in communicating God's love to us. Yet the influence of the Holy Ghost can be obscured by strong emotions, such as anger, hate, . . . [or] fear, . . . like trying to savor the delicate flavor of a grape while eating a jalapeño pepper. . . . [One flavor] completely overpowers the other. So too, behaviors that distance us from the Holy Ghost, including sin, make it difficult for us to perceive God's love for us. . . .
>
> Heavenly Father's prescribed path leads to the best eternal outcomes. We are free to choose, but we cannot choose the consequences of not following the revealed path. The Lord has said, "That which breaketh a law, and abideth not by law, but seeketh to become a law unto itself, . . . cannot be sanctified by law, neither by mercy, justice, nor judgment" (Doctrine and Covenants 88:35). We cannot deviate from Heavenly Father's course and then blame Him for inferior outcomes.[1]

That is exactly what the Lamanites were doing. They were deviating from God's course and then blaming Zeniff for their problems because they didn't understand "the dealings of the Lord" (Mosiah 10:14). Their perception and thus their reality was incorrect and not based in truth.

Self-Reflection:
What is your perception, and is it the reality of truth?

40

BLINDED

"Now the eyes of the people were blinded; therefore they hardened their hearts against the words of Abinadi, and they sought from that time forward to take him. And king Noah hardened his heart against the word of the Lord, and he did not repent of his evil doings." (Mosiah 11:29)

ZENIFF BATTLED THE LAMANITES AGAIN FOR THE THIRD TIME AND beat them, driving them out back to their own lands. He then conferred the kingdom on his son Noah before passing away. Noah did not keep the commandments of God. Instead, he led his people to commit all manner of wickedness, heavily taxing the people to sustain his laziness, idolatry, and iniquity. There arose a prophet among the people by the name of Abinadi, and he prophesied that the people would be brought into bondage if they did not repent and turn from their wickedness. When the people heard him, they were angry and wanted to kill him, but he escaped with the Lord's help (see Mosiah 10–11). "The eyes of the people were blinded" (Mosiah 11:29), and their hearts were hard.

Blinded—what did that look like for them? What would that look like for us? What is spiritual blindness, and what does it mean to have spiritual vision? The following is a story that can shed some light on these questions:

> On May 28, 2016, 16-year-old Beau Richey and his friend Austin were at a family ranch in Colorado. Beau and Austin climbed into their all-terrain vehicles with great anticipation for a day of adventure. They had not gone far when they encountered precarious conditions, at which point tragedy struck. The vehicle Beau was driving flipped over suddenly, pinning Beau under 400 pounds (180 kg) of steel. When Beau's friend Austin got to him, he saw Beau struggling for his life. With every bit of his strength, he tried to pull the vehicle off his friend. It wouldn't budge. He prayed for Beau and then frantically went for help. Emergency personnel finally arrived, but a few hours later Beau died. He was released from this mortal life.
>
> His heartbroken parents arrived. As they stood in the small hospital with Beau's dearest friend and family members, a police officer entered the room and handed Beau's cell phone to his mother. As she took the phone, an audible alarm sounded. She opened the phone and saw Beau's daily alarm. She read aloud the message her fun-loving, highly adventurous teenage son had set to read every day. It said, "Remember to put Jesus Christ at the center of your life today."
>
> Beau's focus on his Redeemer does not lessen his loved ones' sorrow in his absence. However, it gives great hope and meaning to Beau's life and life choices. It allows his family and friends to look beyond only the grief of his early death to the joyful realities of the next life. What a tender mercy for Beau's parents to see through their son's eyes the thing he most prized.[1]

This is spiritual vision: "For he that receiveth my servants receiveth me; And he that receiveth me receiveth my Father; And he that receiveth my Father receiveth my Father's kingdom; therefore all that my Father hath shall be given unto him" (Doctrine and Covenants 84:36–38).

The people of king Noah were blinded. Beau, on the other hand, had the desire to see spiritually as indicated by the reminder on his phone. Do not let your heart be hard, but rather choose to receive Christ in your life and see spiritually.

Self-Reflection:

Set an alarm on your phone to "remember to put Jesus Christ at the center of your life today."

41

COUNTENANCE

*"Now it came to pass after Abinadi had spoken these words that
the people of king Noah durst not lay their hands on him, for
the Spirit of the Lord was upon him; and his face shone with
exceeding luster, even as Moses' did while in the mount of Sinai,
while speaking with the Lord." (Mosiah 13:5)*

TWO YEARS LATER, ABINADI RETURNED TO THE PEOPLE OF KING
Noah and again prophesied to them, following the direction of the
Lord. The people bound him and took him to the king, where he was
thrown into prison. The king assembled his priests to question him,
but to their astonishment, "he did withstand all their questions, and
did confound them in all their words" (Mosiah 12:19). This angered
the king, but as they went to take Abinadi, they were not able "to
lay their hands on him" (Mosiah 13:2) because he had not yet completely delivered the message he was commanded to share from God.
Abinadi's countenance was changed, "for the Spirit of the Lord was
upon him; and his face shone with exceeding luster" (Mosiah 13:5),
and the king and his men would not touch him.

Abinadi was compared to Moses when he returned from talking
with the Lord on Mount Sinai and "the skin of his face shone" so
much that the children of Israel "were afraid to come nigh unto him"

(Exodus 34:29–30), so he had to veil his face before they could speak to him. I marvel at what this may look like as the Spirit of the Lord changes someone so much that their countenance shines and makes them appear different.

In more modern times, we can also read about how the Spirit changes perspective and perception. This occurred after the Church was restored to the earth and the prophet after Joseph Smith was chosen and called.

> After the death of the Prophet Joseph Smith, there was some confusion as to who should lead the Church. Sidney Rigdon, a member of the First Presidency, was among those who claimed to be Joseph's successor. On August 8, 1844, the Lord publicly manifested to the Saints that Brigham Young, President of the Quorum of the Twelve Apostles, was chosen to be the new prophet of the Church. President George Q. Cannon (1827–1901), who later served in the First Presidency, described this miraculous manifestation from the Lord:
>
> > After the martyrdom of the Prophet the Twelve soon returned to Nauvoo, and learned of the aspirations of Sidney Rigdon. He had claimed that the Church needed a guardian, and that he was that guardian. He had appointed the day for the guardian to be selected, and of course, was present at the meeting, which was held in the open air. The wind was blowing toward the stand so strongly at the time that an improvised stand was made out of a wagon, which was drawn up at the back part of the congregation, and which he, [William] Marks, and some others occupied. He attempted to speak, but was much embarrassed. He had been the orator of the Church; but, on this occasion, his oratory failed him, and his talk fell very flat. In the meantime President Young and some of his brethren came and entered the stand. The wind by this time had ceased to blow. After Sidney Rigdon had spoken, President Young arose and addressed the congregation, which faced around to see and hear him, turning their backs towards the wagon occupied by Sidney.
> >
> > It was the first sound of [Brigham's] voice which the people had heard since he had gone east on his mission, and the effect upon them was most wonderful. Who that was present on that occasion can ever forget the impression it made upon them! If Joseph had

risen from the dead and again spoken in their hearing, the effect could not have been more startling than it was to many present at that meeting. It was the voice of Joseph himself; and not only was it the voice of Joseph which was heard; but it seemed in the eyes of the people as though it was the very person of Joseph which stood before them. A more wonderful and miraculous event than was wrought that day in the presence of that congregation we never heard of. The Lord gave His people a testimony that left no room for doubt as to who was the man He had chosen to lead them. They both saw and heard with their natural eyes and ears, and then the words which were uttered came, accompanied by the convincing power of God, to their hearts, and they were filled with the Spirit and with great joy. There had been gloom, and, in some hearts probably, doubt and uncertainty; but now it was plain to all that here was the man upon whom the Lord had bestowed the necessary authority to act in their midst in Joseph's stead.[1]

The Spirit not only changed Brigham Young's voice but also how he appeared to those present on that historic day. The Lord can change us as well, both on the outside and on the inside. He is the source of truth and light.

Self-Reflection:
Have you ever felt your countenance shine or seen another person's countenance shine?

42

STANDING WITH GOD

*"Teach them that redemption cometh through Christ the Lord,
who is the very Eternal Father." (Mosiah 16:15)*

ABINADI IN HIS "SHINING" STATE HAS THE OPPORTUNITY TO TEACH
whatever the Lord needs him to teach. He starts by warning King
Noah and his priests of their idol worship, teaching that they should
only worship the Lord Jesus Christ. Then he teaches them the Ten
Commandments and offers Christ's teachings from the words of
Isaiah. He continues with more testifying of many things regarding
Jesus Christ, including His Resurrection and Atonement. Finally, he
testifies of prophets, repentance, and redemption (see Mosiah 13–16).

Imagine being present for this lengthy sermon and then seeing
Abinadi put to death at King Noah's command. Imagine the power
in that room as he stands there in front of a king and his priests and
the court. There is no fear. He is there to teach of Christ, and the
last words of his sermon testify to His holiness: "redemption cometh
through [Him]" (Mosiah 16:15).

The prophet Abinadi holds a singular place in the Book of Mormon.
He was the first to die as a martyr, and his doctrinal teachings
clarify the purpose of the law of Moses, identify the Redeemer,

and declare facts about the doctrine of resurrection not previously mentioned in the book. He was capable of exquisite language sparked with fiery metaphor, yet was plainspoken to the point of bluntness.

Abinadi confronted the wicked establishment single-handedly. The record gives no hint of any other prophet being present with him. So far as we know, he converted but one man, yet that one man (Alma) became the progenitor of a posterity that kept the sacred records and served as the ecclesiastical leaders (and sometimes the political leaders) for the remainder of the Nephite history, a period of well over four hundred years. Without Abinadi's story, the Book of Mormon would lack continuity, and a major part of the book's message would be missing.[1]

As Elder D. Todd Christofferson described, "Abinadi was intent on fulfilling his divine commission. 'I finish my message,' he said, 'and then it matters not [what happens to me], if it so be that I am saved.' He was not spared a martyr's death, but assuredly he was saved in the kingdom of God, and his one precious convert, Alma, changed the course of Nephite history leading up to the coming of Christ."[2] Alma was one of King Noah's priests who fled from the court to escape his own death, experienced his own conversion to Christ, and preached the words of Abinadi (see Mosiah 17:2–4).

I imagine what might have gone through Abinadi's head as he spent his last breath preaching to a wicked king and his people who would not listen to him before sending him to a death by fire. Yet this moment in history—seemingly a failure with only one convert—changed the course of many generations of people, encouraging them to love and follow Jesus Christ. This is what Abinadi's last words were about. Alma heard them and (literally) ran with it. Abinadi is a revered and beloved prophet now by millions of God's children—including me.

"May we ever be courageous and prepared to stand for what we believe, and if we must stand alone in the process, may we do so courageously, strengthened by the knowledge that in reality we are never alone when we stand with our Father in Heaven."[3]

Self-Reflection:
Can you think of a time in your life when the power of
someone's example strengthened you?

43

WHERE ARE WE LEARNING?

*"And also trust no one to be your teacher nor your minister,
except he be a man of God, walking in his ways and keeping
his commandments. . . . And it came to pass that none received
authority to preach or to teach except it were by him from
God. . . . and none were consecrated except they were just men."*
(Mosiah 23:14, 17)

AFTER HEARING ABINADI'S POWERFUL SERMON, ALMA "REPENTED OF
his sins and iniquities and went about privately among the people, and
began to preach the words of Abinadi" (Mosiah 18:1). He then baptized many converts to the gospel in "the waters of Mormon" (Mosiah
18:8)—about 204 people (see Mosiah 18:16)—and organized the
Church of Christ. Eventually, King Noah heard about what was going on among his people and "sent his army to destroy them" (Mosiah
18:33), prompting Alma and his people to depart into the wilderness
and eventually settle their own city called Helam.

In Helam, the people grew and prospered, and Alma reminded
them that since "they were delivered by the power of God . . . they
should stand fast in this liberty wherewith [they had] been made free."
(Mosiah 23:13) Further, he instructed the Church of Christ about
where they should receive their teachings from, telling them to "trust

no one to be your teacher . . . except he be a man of God" (Mosiah 23:14).

I wonder how *we* are receiving our teachings, or from where we get our information to gain knowledge and form our opinions. Is it from God and just men and women, or is it from someone or somewhere else? Maybe TV, Facebook, politicians, or cable news?

President Nelson has given wise counsel on this subject, teaching the following:

"As we seek to be disciples of Jesus Christ, our efforts to *hear Him* need to be ever more intentional. It takes conscious and consistent effort to fill our daily lives with His words, His teachings, His truths. We simply cannot rely upon information we bump into on social media. With billions of words online and in a marketing-saturated world constantly infiltrated by noisy, nefarious efforts of the adversary."[1]

"If most of the information you get comes from social or other media, your ability to hear the whisperings of the Spirit will be diminished. If you are not also seeking the Lord through daily prayer and gospel study, you leave yourself vulnerable to philosophies that may be intriguing but are not true. Even Saints who are otherwise faithful can be derailed by the steady beat of Babylon's band."[2]

"The voices and pressures of the world are engaging and numerous. But too many voices are deceptive, seductive, and can pull us off the covenant path. To avoid the inevitable heartbreak that follows, I plead with you today to counter the lure of the world by making time for the Lord in your life—each and every day."[2]

Over the last year, I have removed myself off every social media outlet except one that I use for job searches and networking. It has been very hard to do. I began feeling the desire to distance myself from social media two years ago as I felt myself being sucked into a constant drive to be scrolling through post after post wasting time. I felt like the engaging, numerous, deceptive, addictive, and seductive desires to surf the net, scroll my current feed, or watch the latest news was pulling me away from the covenant path where I wished to be.

After a year off social media, I still sometimes yearn to know what is happening in the world of my social media accounts—what's happening with my "friends" or on my favorite pages. The pull is strong, but little by little the desire lessens. I went through a period of withdrawal that included very dark thoughts and anxiety, much like with other addictions I have fought before to overcome. It has been added to a list of issues that I strive daily to lay at the feet of my Savior. I think that for some, social media can be a positive spiritual outlet if they are focused, but that line got blurred too quickly for me to manage.

I'm reminded of President Nelson's words: "The adversary is clever. For millennia he has been making good look evil and evil look good. His messages tend to be loud, bold, and boastful. However, messages from our Heavenly Father are strikingly different. He communicates simply, quietly, and with such stunning plainness that we cannot misunderstand Him."[1]

This helps me to understand better the fine lines of how and where we are receiving our teachings. Again, I share, "As we seek to be disciples of Jesus Christ, our efforts to hear Him need to be ever more intentional. It takes conscious and consistent effort to fill our daily lives with His words, His teachings, His truths."[3]

Self-Reflection:
How easy is it for you to use your favorite social media app and not cross the blurred line of seeing good as evil and evil as good?

44

Prayer in the Heart

*"And Alma and his people did not raise their voices to the Lord
their God, but did pour out their hearts to him; and he did
know the thoughts of their hearts." (Mosiah 24:12)*

ALMA AND THE PEOPLE OF THE CHURCH OF CHRIST WERE EVENTU-
ally found by the Lamanites. After crying unto the Lord for help, "the
Lord did soften the hearts of the Lamanites" to spare their lives, but
Alma's people still had to "[deliver] themselves up into their hands;
and the Lamanites took possession of the land of Helam" (Mosiah
23:29).

The Lamanites also found the priests of Noah, who were now led
by a man named Amulon, "and Amulon and his brethren did join the
Lamanites" (Mosiah 23:35) after being spared from destruction. The
king of the Lamanites "granted unto Amulon that he should be a king
and a ruler over his people . . . nevertheless he should have no power
to do anything contrary to the will of the king of the Lamanites"
(Mosiah 23:39).

Amulon "did gain favor in the eyes of the king of the Lamanites"
(Mosiah 24:1) and "began to exercise authority over Alma and his
brethren, and began to persecute him" (Mosiah 24:8). This is because
Amulon knew that Alma had been a priest of King Noah and had

"believed the words of Abinadi and was driven out" (Mosiah 24:9). Amulon did not like him. He exercised authority over him and his people, and "so great were their afflictions that they began to cry mightily to God" (Mosiah 24:10). Amulon ordered them to "stop their cries; and he put guards over them to watch them, that whosoever should be found calling upon God should be put to death" (Mosiah 24:11).

This left the people of Alma with no other choice than to "pour out their hearts to him" (Mosiah 24:12), without raising their voices, to deliver them from their bondage. God listened, "and he did know the thoughts of their hearts" (Mosiah 24:12). Soon He "caused a deep sleep to come upon the Lamanites" (Mosiah 24:19) so that Alma and his people could all escape (even with their flocks) and go to the land of Zarahemla. Twelve days later they arrived, and "king Mosiah did also receive them with joy" (Mosiah 24:25).

Praying in your heart and pouring out your thoughts to God in silence works—He hears them. As I sit here writing this chapter, I have searched the scriptures, conference talks, and *Liahona* articles for a compelling story to share. Then, as I said yet another prayer in my heart for guidance and direction, it hit me—I should share my own experience with praying silently right now.

Before I read each verse and study the background for context to share at the beginning of each topic, I silently pray in my heart to my Father in Heaven for His guidance. As I was stuck with this entry, wanting to express a compelling story, I prayed again and had the thought to share about writing this book. I have prayed hundreds (maybe thousands) of times while writing throughout my life. I could not do it without prayer. I love that God knows my thoughts when I pray, addressing them directly to Him.

I have found that as I've prayed continually, learned to listen to thoughts and impressions, and honed in on my spiritual instincts, I have been guided by the Holy Ghost in my life. Yesterday, I was taking a walk with Diony through the woods next to my home, in a large intersecting trail system, and I was leading the way. While we hiked, I prayed in my heart several times to know which direction the Lord would have me choose as I approached various intersections in the path. I knew where each trail led and was not lost; however, I didn't know which one the Lord would have me take that day.

At each junction, I had a clear impression—or, more accurately, a visualization—of which one to take. The route ended up being very different than what I had planned originally. Why did the Lord want me to choose that particular route? I don't know. I just felt like it was right. I had the impression that as I do more silent praying of this type—and then listen—it will strengthen my ability to follow His path for me in the future, similar to strengthening a muscle by lifting heavy weights. I *can* strengthen my ability to listen. I want that.

I most often hear the Lord as a voice in my thoughts or as a feeling of peace, joy, energy, or understanding—and now, most recently, with visions in my mind. I love that the Lord is increasing my ability to listen as I strive to hear Him.

Self-Reflection:

What are the ways that you hear Him? What are some new ways you want to hear Him?

45

A Chance

*"And he became a great hinderment to the prosperity of the
church of God; stealing away the hearts of the people; causing
much dissension among the people; giving a chance for the
enemy of God to exercise his power over them." (Mosiah 27:9)*

"AFTER NEARLY THREE GENERATIONS OF LIVING IN SEPARATE LANDS,
the Nephites were one people again."[1] This included the people of
King Mosiah, the people of Alma, and the people of King Limhi,
and even though they were not all descended from Nephi, they "were
numbered with the Nephites" (Mosiah 25:13). King Mosiah gathered
them all together and spoke to them, and after he finished, "he desired
that Alma should also speak to the people. . . . They were assembled together in large bodies, and he went from one body to another,
preaching unto the people repentance and faith on the Lord" (Mosiah
25:14–15). After listening, Limhi and his people desired to be baptized, and King Mosiah granted unto Alma that he might establish
the Church of Christ throughout all the land of Zarahemla. "And
they were called the people of God" (Mosiah 25:24).

Over the next twenty years and beyond, many "of the rising generation" who had been children when King Benjamin gave his powerful sermon "did not believe the traditions of their fathers" (Mosiah

26:1), began to persecute the Church, and started doing all manner of iniquity in Zarahemla. Some of the loudest dissenters were "the sons of [King] Mosiah . . . and also one of the sons of Alma . . . he being called Alma, after his father" (Mosiah 27:8). Alma the Younger was in such opposition to his father's teachings that he "became a great hinderment to the prosperity of the church of God; stealing away the hearts of the people; causing much dissension among the people; giving a chance for the enemy of God to exercise his power over them" (Mosiah 27:9–10).

I think the wording is very interesting in this verse when it says that because of the dissension he caused among the people, it gave "a chance" for the devil to exercise his power over them. If Alma the Younger had not stolen away the hearts of the people, causing the dissension, would they not have faltered? Would Satan not have had a chance to exercise his power? I'm not sure.

I know that one of the reasons we are sent to this earth is to be tested "to see if [we] will do all things whatsoever the Lord [our] God shall command" (Abraham 3:25) so that we may return to Him. Maybe this desire to destroy the Church was one of Alma the Younger's tests, and maybe it was a test for the Church as well.

I believe in the principle of momentum, and if there is movement heading in a specific direction, it can be hard to stop. Let's consider for a minute what President Nelson taught about momentum:

> *Momentum* is a powerful concept. We all have experienced it in one form or another—for example, in a vehicle that picks up speed or with a disagreement that suddenly turns into an argument.
>
> So I ask, what can ignite *spiritual momentum*? We have seen examples of both positive and negative momentum. We know followers of Jesus Christ who became converted and grew in their faith. But we also know of once-committed believers who fell away. Momentum can swing either way.
>
> We have never needed *positive* spiritual momentum more than we do now, to counteract the speed with which evil and the darker signs of the times are intensifying. Positive spiritual momentum will keep us moving forward amid the fear and uncertainty created by pandemics, tsunamis, volcanic eruptions, and armed hostilities. Spiritual momentum can help us withstand the relentless, wicked

attacks of the adversary and thwart his efforts to erode our personal spiritual foundation.[2]

This sounds exactly like what Alma the Younger was allowing Satan to do—erode the spiritual foundations of himself, his friends, and the dissenters of the Church. We must fortify ourselves and not give him that "chance."

President Nelson taught, "The antidote to Satan's scheme is clear: we need daily experiences worshipping the Lord and studying His gospel. I plead with you to let God prevail in your life. Give Him a fair share of your time. As you do, notice what happens to your positive spiritual momentum."[1]

Thankfully, Alma the Younger was not a "hinderment" to the Church for long, because in this chapter, we also learn that he and the sons of Mosiah—Ammon, Aaron, Himni, and Omner—had a miraculous visit from an "angel of the Lord" (Mosiah 27:11) calling them to repentance. After a time of being struck dumb, Alma "repented of [his] sins," (Mosiah 27:24) converted to the Lord, and served His people. The rest of his life, he tried to rectify the damage he had caused to the Church and became a great leader and prophet—an instrument "in the hands of God in bringing many to the knowledge of the truth" (Mosiah 27:36).

Alma the Younger found his positive spiritual momentum.

Self-Reflection:

What is one thing you can do today to close the door to the adversary and gain positive spiritual momentum?

PART IX

THE BOOK OF ALMA
(ABOUT 91–53 BC)

"The Book of Mormon was written for us today. God is the author of the book. It is a record of a fallen people, compiled by inspired men for our blessing today.... [The Book of Mormon] was meant for us."

—President Ezra Taft Benson[1]

46

STAND FAST

"Now this was a great trial to those that did stand fast in the faith; nevertheless, they were steadfast and immovable in keeping the commandments of God, and they bore with patience the persecution which was heaped upon them." (Alma 1:25)

THE BOOK OF ALMA BEGINS AFTER THE PEOPLE DECIDED TO BE DONE being ruled by kings. Instead, judges are appointed to govern according to the law. Alma the Younger is appointed to be "the first chief judge" and "the high priest" over the Church (Mosiah 29:42), obeying "the ways of the Lord" (Mosiah 29:43). It had been 509 years since Lehi left Jerusalem.

During the first year of the reign of the judges, a man named Nehor introduced priestcraft, which is defined as when people "preach and set themselves up for a light unto the world, that they may get gain and praise of the world; but they seek not the welfare of Zion" (2 Nephi 26:29). Nehor committed murder and was condemned to die. But after his death, priestcraft continued, and those who didn't belong to the Church persecuted those that did. The persecution of the Church caused "great trial to those that did stand fast in the faith; nevertheless they were steadfast and immovable in keeping the commandments of God, and they bore the persecution which was heaped upon them" (Alma 1:25).

In our day, as we face persecution of different kinds for being followers of Christ, we too must "stand fast" in our faith, be immovable in keeping the commandments, and be patient in affliction. We can do this by holding on to our covenants—those we made at baptism and those we make in the temple. Our covenants make us belong.

In a world that shouts to us different definitions of what belonging means, we can recognize the false labels as a mirage or illusion and can clearly see through them when we turn to the words of our prophet. President Nelson said, "If any label replaces your most important identifiers, the result can be spiritually suffocating. I believe that if the Lord were speaking to you directly, the first thing He would make sure you understand is your true identity . . . [as a] Child of God, Child of the Covenant, [and] Disciple of Jesus Christ. Any identifier that is not compatible with those three basic designations will ultimately let you down."[1]

As we commit to keeping our covenants and following Jesus Christ, we will absolutely be met with opposition, "for it must needs be, that there is an opposition in all things" (2 Nephi 2:11), and it might even come from those we love. But that doesn't mean we should turn away from the truth. We also learn from the scriptures, "That which doth not edify is not of God, and is darkness. That which is of God is light; and he that receiveth light, and continueth in God, receiveth more light" (Doctrine and Covenants 50:23–24).

I've experienced this in my own life as I've prayed to Heavenly Father to discern truth from error. The Spirit confirms truth by filling me with peace and calmness—a vivid contrast to feelings of fear, turmoil, and darkness. In this way, I've been able to recognize deception, turn away from it, and hold fast to my covenants.

Sister Jean B. Bingham said:

I have been continually assured that keeping the covenants we make with God allows us to draw upon the Savior's power, which strengthens us in our inevitable trials, provides protection from the adversary's influence, and prepares us for eternal glory.

Many of us are experiencing rough waters. As we are tossed by waves of adversity and are sometimes blinded by the torrents of tears that come in those difficulties, we may not know which direction to paddle our life boat. We may not even think we have the strength to get to shore. Remembering who you are—a beloved child of God—why you are on the earth, and your goal of living with God and your loved ones can clear your vision and point you in the right direction. In the midst of the storm there is a bright light to show the way.[2]

I know and testify that that bright light is our Savior Jesus Christ—"the light that shineth in darkness" (Doctrine and Covenants 6:21).

Self-Reflection:
Are you standing fast on the covenant path?

47

CHANGED HEARTS

"Have ye spiritually been born of God? Have ye received his image in your countenances? Have ye experienced this mighty change in your hearts?" (Alma 5:14)

IN THIS CHAPTER, ALMA HAD RECENTLY APPOINTED A NEW CHIEF judge, Nephihah, to govern the people so that he could go forth among his people and preach the word of God. Over the last several years, he watched contentions among the people of the Church increase, and he wanted "to stir them up in remembrance of their duty" (Alma 4:19), starting in the city of Zarahemla, the cultural capital of the Nephites. He reminded them of what happened to their fathers and how God "changed their hearts; yea, he awakened them out of a deep sleep. . . . They were in the midst of darkness; nevertheless, their souls were illuminated by the light of the everlasting word" (Alma 5:7).

After Alma gave more details of what had happened to their fathers, the conditions of how they were saved, and the mighty changes that occurred in their hearts, he asked the people he was teaching if they had "spiritually been born of God" (Alma 5:14).

Alma's speech is very much for our day as well, for when we choose to follow Christ, we choose to be changed. "The Lord works from the inside out. The world works from the outside in. The world would mold people by changing their environment. Christ changes men, who then change their environment. The world would shape human behavior, but Christ can change human nature."[1]

The Lord can change hearts. He can change attitudes. He can change dispositions. He can help us be different—more like Him—and filled with peace, compassion, and understanding, especially toward others. But this is a process that sometimes includes difficult lessons.

A stake president experienced this humbling process of change when on one busy day in particular, his plans to be spiritually in tune for an upcoming evening of interviews and important meetings fell apart. He had to go to several places of business to get something fixed, and his impatience grew as nothing went smoothly. Negative feelings toward the employees of the businesses magnified as he mentally reasoned, "Why can't people just be competent in their jobs and do things properly the first time?" Soon he found himself angry, frustrated, and in a state of high anxiety.

As the time grew closer for him to fulfill the duties of his calling, he called on Heavenly Father and pleaded for help to feel His Spirit. He wanted to be meek, but still he felt no relief from his distraught feelings of the difficult day. He asked for grace, mercy, and forgiveness, but nothing changed. On his drive to the stake center, he continued praying, not knowing what else to do. Finally, as he entered the doors of the building, he heard a voice in his heart and mind, saying, "President, you ask Me for grace and mercy. You could have been gracious."

He felt ashamed. He knew he could have and should have done better. He repented more fervently and was inspired by ways he could better bless those he had wronged. He was filled with joy when the Spirit of the Lord finally touched his heart—and changed it—giving him peace of conscience.[2]

A sister shared that she always feels the Spirit when she reads this scripture in Alma 5:14. She asks herself, "Have *I* been spiritually born of God?" Many may think this scripture is about having a testimony, but she sees it as being truly converted.

Do we give our *whole* life to the Lord, or just the easy parts?

Have we received His image in our countenance?

Have our hearts been changed?

She thinks of a patriarch she knows in whom she sees the Savior every time she looks at him. Others have told her they see something in *her* that sets her apart from others. She hopes she has enough faith in the Lord Jesus Christ to do what is asked of her, and that He can depend on her to be His hands here on earth. She hopes she is ready to face Him when the time comes, and that her words and deeds reflect His example. She feels His love more abundantly when she is serving others. She hears His voice most often in the quiet of the early morning and tries to listen and follow what He tells her.

Like Alma 5:16 says, "Can you imagine to yourselves that ye hear the voice of the Lord saying unto you, in that day: Come unto me ye blessed, for behold, your works have been works of righteousness upon the face of the earth?" Someday, she hopes to experience this, and as she stands before Him, she wants to be able to say that she has done all she could to be like Him.

As we study the truths within the Book of Mormon, we can hear the Savior's voice more clearly for ourselves, just like the above two examples illustrate.

Self-Reflection:
Can others see Jesus Christ reflected in you?

48

He Understands

"And he shall go forth, suffering pains and afflictions and temptations of every kind; and this that the word might be fulfilled. . . . that he might blot out their transgressions according to the power of his deliverance." (Alma 7:11, 13)

Alma is now teaching in the valley of Gideon, being led by the Spirit regarding what those people most needed to hear. He preached to them repentance, exhorting them to prepare for the coming of the Lord Jesus Christ, who would be born of a virgin in "the land of [their] forefathers" (Alma 7:10). He expounded that Christ would loose the bands of death and take upon Him the people's sins with mercy so they could be delivered from their transgressions.

That gift—Christ's grace and mercy—was for them, you, and me.

Have you ever felt like no one truly comprehends what you may be struggling with or facing? Have those feelings made you feel misunderstood and alone? Through the scriptures, the words of the prophets, and faith, we can know that *He* knows exactly what we feel, experience, suffer, and endure. Alma tells us that Christ suffered "pains and afflictions and temptations of every kind" (Alma 7:11).

That means Jesus knows what it felt like when my father died in an airplane crash when I was seven years old, and how Trent felt watching his first wife die from cancer. He knows exactly what *they* went through, and He knows how it still feels for *us*. He knows how scared our daughter was when she got on the wrong bus after school and ended up lost in a strange neighborhood. He knows how our son felt when he got bullied online by a girl he broke up with. He knows what it's like to be a victim of abuse, to struggle with addiction, and to lose everything in a bad financial decision. He knows the pain of a broken heart when your spouse is unfaithful, and the rejection you feel when you're overlooked for a deserved promotion at work. He knows what it feels like to believe death is the answer instead of living, and He knows the sorrow and sadness those left behind feel when suicide takes their loved one away. He knows the discouragement and exhaustion caused by ongoing chronic pain and the misunderstood shame of mental illness.

"The Savior has suffered not just for our sins and iniquities—but also for our physical pains and anguish, our weaknesses and short-comings, our fears and frustrations, our disappointments and discour-agements, our regrets and remorse, our despair and desperation, the injustices and inequities we experience, and the emotional distresses that beset us. There is no physical pain, no spiritual wound, no an-guish of soul or heartache, no infirmity or weakness you or I ever confront in mortality that the Savior did not experience first."[1]

Jesus Christ, our Savior, knows and understands it all.

Self-Reflection:
Is there something you are trying to carry alone that you should give to Christ?

49

HEAR AND HEARKEN

"Nevertheless, I did harden my heart, for I was called many times and I would not hear . . . therefore I went on rebelling against God. . . . [But] as I was journeying to see a very near kindred, behold an angel of the Lord appeared unto me and said: Amulek, return to thine own house, for thou shalt feed a prophet of the Lord." (Alma 10:6–7)

THE BACKSTORY TO THE SCRIPTURES WE ARE FOCUSING ON IN THIS chapter, Alma 10, begins in chapter 8. Alma was continuing his preaching and had recently been in the land of Melek, west of the river Sidon. After he finished baptizing there, he journeyed for three days to the north and came to the land of Ammonihah to teach and prophesy. The people of Ammonihah would not listen—their hearts were hard. Alma "labored much in spirit" (Alma 8:10) and wrestled with God through mighty prayer that the people in that city would be touched so they would repent and be baptized, but they "reviled him, spit upon him, and caused that he should be cast out of their city" (Alma 8:12). He left with a heavy heart and much anguish because of their wickedness.

On his way to the city of Aaron, "an angel of the Lord appeared" (Alma 8:14), commending him for his faithfulness and commanding him to return again to Ammonihah. This time, he was to tell the people that if they didn't repent, they would be destroyed. Alma obeyed and returned. The Lord prepared a way for Alma to receive support and follow His will through a Nephite named Amulek.

Amulek had struggled in the past to listen to God, but this time "an angel of the Lord appeared unto [him]" (Alma 10:7). God sent that angel in a vision to Amulek to tell him to take in Alma and give him food, promising Amulek that his obedience would bring blessings. Amulek was a Nephite by birth, had a solid reputation among his peers, and was wealthy. He admitted that even though he had seen God's mysteries and power, he didn't know much of His ways because his heart was hard.

As we study this account, we see that God didn't give up on Amulek, and He doesn't give up on us if we will hear Him and "hearken." Amulek finally recognized God was in his life, and he said, "For behold, he hath blessed mine house, he hath blessed me, and my women, and my children, and my father, and my kinsfolk; yea even all my kindred hath he blessed" (Alma 10:11).

God called Amulek to a great work—to teach and testify with Alma as another witness of Jesus Christ and to bring others to repentance and baptism. And Amulek listened.

A brother shared his thoughts about why Amulek inspires him. This man, like many of us, sometimes hears God but doesn't always listen. In this account, Amulek had an experience that turned his attention to God—seeing the angel, then being told to find Alma and receive him into his house—and following those instructions changed Amulek's life.

Amulek became faithful in listening to and following future promptings and directions from God. He learned about the gospel and then went with Alma to teach the gospel, "and the people began to be astonished, seeing there was more than one witness who testified" (Alma 10:12). The Lord needed Amulek's credibility. As Amulek taught, he learned he could trust God to give him understanding and the "right words" to speak to the people of Ammonihah. Amulek experienced several different ways God uses to speak to us.

Through reading and studying this scriptural account, this brother learned that thoughts, impressions, feelings, scriptures, and prophets are some of the ways that God can speak to *him*.

The last verse of this song by Gerald Lund sums it up well:

> I must hear and hearken,
> Read, and then obey.
> I must pray and ponder,
> Then walk within his way.
> It is not enough to read,
> To lay hold upon the word.
> Not until I give full heed,
> Will he know I have heard.[1]

Self-Reflection:
Do you recognize the Lord when He speaks to you?

50

In His Strength I Can Do All Things

"Yea, I know that I am nothing: as to my strength I am weak;
therefore I will not boast of myself, but I will boast of my God,
for in his strength I can do all things." (Alma 26:12)

In this chapter, Ammon—along with his brothers Aaron, Omner, and Himni, whose conversion story we learned about in the book of Mosiah—are discussing "how great reason we have to rejoice" (Alma 26:1). This is in regard to their missionary efforts with thousands of Lamanites who "have been brought into the fold of God" (Alma 26:4).

At one point in the conversation, Ammon says, "If we had not come up out of the land of Zarahemla, these our dearly beloved brethren . . . would still be racked with hatred against us, yea, and they would also have been strangers to God" (Alma 26:9). After this comment, Aaron rebuked Ammon, saying, "I fear that thy joy doth carry thee away unto boasting" (Alma 26:10).

Ammon quickly clarified that he was not boasting of his own strength or wisdom: "Yea, I know that I am nothing: as to my strength

I am weak; therefore I will not boast of myself, but I will boast of my God, for in his strength I can do all things" (Alma 26:12).

Ammon's joy was coming from God because he knows that he is nothing without Him.

I absolutely love this scripture! It is definitely one of my favorites in the Book of Mormon. So many times I have taken these words of Ammon to heart and found the courage to do whatever I needed that seemed too scary, difficult, or maybe even impossible—because I knew that with God's strength, I could find a way to do it, especially when it was something He was asking of me. When I've trusted in Him and moved forward doing my best, He has always opened up the way and made up the difference that I lack. Every time I have felt Him with me, my love and faith in Him has grown and I learn I truly can trust Him in all things. And when I forget, He reminds me.

This happened on a recent visit to the Church history sites of Nauvoo with Trent.

It was a chilly November morning with intermittent rain. I was grateful for my long warm coat and gloves, especially on the ox wagon tour. Our tour guides were a sweet missionary couple, both dressed in historical clothing. While the brother led the oxen on the tour, his wife narrated, walking beside the wagon as Trent and I rode, jostled along by the uneven terrain.

She talked about the oxen, giving us more detail on their mannerisms and use by the early Saints. The oxen pair pulling our wagon were yoked together, side by side. She discussed the importance of the yoking, especially when one of the oxen is weaker than the other, because the stronger ox of the two can help compensate for the weakness of the other, creating a more solid team of two. She likened those oxen to us and the Savior. When we are yoked with Him, our weaknesses and struggles are compensated by His strength, and with that strength we can do and face whatever He asks of us.

A warm feeling coursed through my heart at her words, causing my eyes to fill with tears. I was reminded clearly that He was aware of me. He was aware of my struggling with the recent trials in my life and specific choices He had guided me to make that I didn't completely understand. I was grateful to be reminded that as I leaned on Him, my load would be lightened enough to bear.

"God invites us to respond with faith . . . in order that we may reap blessings and gain knowledge that can be learned in no other way."[1]

"He is our perfect Father. He loves us beyond our capacity to understand. He knows what is best for us. He sees the end from the beginning. He wants us to act to gain needed experience."[2]

The New Testament has a similar scripture to the one in Alma—I love it too! It says, "I can do all things through Christ which strengtheneth me" (Philippians 4:13).

Self-Reflection:
Is there something in your life you can commit to find the courage to face with God?

51

His Timing, Not Ours

"Yea, he that repenteth and exerciseth faith, and bringeth forth good works, and prayeth continually without ceasing—unto such it is given to know the mysteries of God." (Alma 26:22)

JUST A LITTLE FURTHER IN THE SAME CHAPTER, ALMA 26, A DIFFERent scripture stood out to someone else. One sister shared the following.

She distinctly remembers opening to Alma 26:22 during a very difficult time in her life. She was so frustrated because she could not understand why God was allowing the anguish she faced.

She was fourteen years old at the time, and she was asking significant questions that were tough for her to answer:

Was she being abused?

Did God even care about her?

Why was He letting this happen?

Was it her fault?

Looking back years later, she cherishes His direct response to her questions. Instead of allowing her to just wallow in despair, He told her what she must do to learn why this was happening—repent, exercise faith, serve others, pray continually, and endure in her trial. After she put in the effort, He would one day reveal why this challenge was so prevalent in her life.

She didn't like His answer! She wanted Him to resolve the issue and tell her she was right. Instead, she realized He had a marvelous lesson for her to learn, and over the course of several years, by applying His counsel, she gained more insight into what she had asked.

Was she being abused?

The question weighed heavily on her mind as she went back and forth between the dictionary definitions and painful feelings that she buried deeper and deeper. Today, that question no longer haunts her because the answer doesn't define her worth, and she no longer allows it to define the other person she sees. Instead, she sees a loving God who kindly encouraged her to choose forgiveness and view all His children more clearly through His eyes.

Did God even care about her?

Absolutely, one hundred percent. This is a principle she's still learning. He cared for her so much that He let her suffer in order to learn. She can empathize, be a support, and share her story with others to validate them, and she can understand her true value as a daughter of a perfect eternal Father.

Why was He letting this happen?

He doesn't interfere in agency, and others' actions sometimes unfairly affect our own. He allowed her to grieve and mourn over what could have been and what the outcome was of her childhood, and all of those burdensome experiences helped her become who she is today. He allowed her to feel deep pain so she would turn to Him and better understand when others feel their own pain.

Was it her fault?

No, what happened was not her fault. But that answer alone didn't solve the past or help her come to terms with her grief. Because we are all accountable for our personal actions, she was reminded of the ways she reacted that she could have handled differently. However, she's learned it's not about blame. It's about love, acceptance, repentance, healing, growing, and trusting her Savior—and, most importantly, letting go of others' wrongdoings to enable God to forgive her for hers.

In this chapter, Ammon is expressing gratitude for the remarkable change God has wrought upon the Lamanites. Thousands have come unto God, repented, and become new creatures. It's beautiful, poetic, and deeply illustrative of the joy that comes from redemption of each person's soul.

As this sister heeded the counsel she received from this passage, she truly came unto God. She absolutely found joy amidst her darkest moments and came to understand His perfect plan and why her adversity was so necessary. She learned a wise lesson—that His timing is different from ours—and she is so grateful that she could hear Him clearly through the scriptures.

> ### Self-Reflection:
> *As you read this chapter in the Book of Mormon, what verses stand out to you and why?*

52

Nourish the Seed

"If ye give place, that a seed may be planted in your heart, behold, if it be a true seed, or a good seed, if ye do not cast it out by your unbelief . . . it will begin to swell . . . and when you feel these swelling motions, ye will begin to say within yourselves—It must be . . . good, for it beginneth to enlarge my soul; yea, it beginneth to enlighten my understanding, yea, it beginneth to be delicious to me." (Alma 32:28)

ALMA IS TEACHING THE ZORAMITES (DISSENTERS FROM THE Nephites) in a place called Antionum. Some of their beliefs and practices astonished Alma and his brethren. Their method of prayer occurred only once a week and was vain and repetitive, and many of their beliefs were prideful, worldly, and anti-Christ. Alma and his brethren pleaded in prayer that they would be guided as missionaries to help them.

The poor among them, the ones who had not been permitted to enter the synagogue, were troubled because they had no place to worship. Alma "beheld that their afflictions had truly humbled them, and that they were in a preparation to hear the word" (Alma 32:6). Because they were in a humble state, Alma and his brethren were able to teach them many things. In his teachings, he was able to share a discourse on faith in the word of God, teaching that if they were willing to start with a small amount—even just the "desire to believe" what he was telling them—it could start to grow in their heart like a newly planted seed. If they continued to nurture it and "not cast it out," it would eventually become "delicious" to them (see Alma 32:27–28).

Growing and developing faith, which Alma compares to a seed, is a conscious choice. Bishop Richard C. Edgley taught:

> Faith is not a free gift given without thought, desire, or effort. It does not come as the dew falls from heaven. The Savior said, "Come unto me," and "Knock, and it shall be [given] you." These are action verbs—*come, knock.* They are choices. [We can] choose faith over doubt, choose faith over fear, choose faith over the unknown and the unseen, and choose faith over pessimism. . . .
>
> Alma gave us a directive to choose. . . . He used the words *awake, arouse, experiment, exercise, desire, work,* and *plant.* Then Alma explained that if we make these choices and do not cast the seed out by unbelief, then "it will begin to swell within [our] breasts" (Alma 32:28).[1]

The chapter continues to discuss the importance of staying humble during this process of growth. As the Holy Ghost witnesses of truth, the seed—or faith in the word of God—grows. As faith is held on to, roots develop and then the tree. Alma gives us the formula, as Bishop Edgley explained:

> If confusion and hopelessness weigh on your mind, *choose* to "awake and arouse your faculties" (Alma 32:27). Humbly approaching the Lord with a broken heart and contrite spirit is the pathway to truth and the Lord's way of light, knowledge, and peace.
>
> If your testimony is immature, untested, and insecure, *choose* to "exercise [even] a particle of faith"; *choose* to experiment upon [His] words" (Alma 32:27). The Savior explained, "If any man will do his will, he shall know of the doctrine, whether it be of God, or whether I speak of myself" (John 7:17).
>
> When logic, reason, or personal intellect come into conflict with sacred teachings and doctrine, or conflicting messages assault your beliefs as the fiery darts described by the Apostle Paul (see Ephesians 6:16), *choose* to not cast the seed out of your heart by

unbelief. Remember, we receive not a witness until after the trial of our faith (see Ether 12:6).[2]

With continued nourishment and patience, eventually spiritual fruit is harvested: "Fruit which is most precious, which is sweet above all that is sweet, and which is white above all that is white, yea, and pure above all that is pure; and ye shall feast upon this fruit even until ye are filled, that ye hunger not, neither shall ye thirst" (Alma 32:42).

Just like the Zoramites, we too are on our own journey of gaining a solid and fruitful testimony in our hearts of Jesus Christ and His gospel, leading us ultimately to receive eternal life.

President Eyring said this about that journey: "You have felt the quiet confirmation in your heart and mind that something was true. And you knew that it was inspiration from God. It may have come during a talk, lesson, or hymn in church. The Holy Ghost is the Spirit of Truth. You feel peace, hope, and joy when He speaks to your heart and mind that something is true. Almost always I have also felt a sensation of light. Any feeling of darkness is dispelled, and my desire to do right grows."[3]

Trent's and my journey so far has not been smooth and straight. In fact, we both have had to scale some pretty intense mountain cliffs. But along the way, our personal fortitude and determination to continue forward has grown stronger. Daily heartfelt prayer and feasting on the word of God through conference talks and the scriptures (especially the Book of Mormon), alone and as a couple, has invited the Spirit into our home more than anything else.

But just like you, we still are growing and can always do better, which makes us so grateful our God is patient with us, letting us learn to "glory in tribulations also; knowing tribulation worketh patience; and patience experience; and experience, hope" (Romans 5:3–4).

Self-Reflection:
What is one thing you can commit to do better this week to nourish your testimony?

53

IN THEE IS MY JOY

"And thou didst hear me because of mine afflictions and my sincerity; and it is because of thy Son that thou hast been merciful unto me, therefore I will cry unto thee in all mine afflictions, for in thee is my joy." (Alma 33:11)

THIS CHAPTER BEGINS WITH ALMA SHARING THE TEACHINGS OF Zenos, a prophet of ancient Israel whose words were lost from the Old Testament. Zenos is mentioned in several different books in the Book of Mormon. In these verses, Alma is quoting Zenos on the subject of prayer. Zenos said God heard his prayers in the wilderness, in the fields, in his home, in his closet, in the midst of congregations, during times he was cast out and despised, and during times of afflictions. He said this occurs through God's mercy because of His Son, Jesus Christ. In sincerity, Zenos then says, "Therefore I will cry unto thee in all my afflictions, for in thee is my joy" (Alma 33:11).

A sister relates to this, saying she loves how Alma teaches that we can find joy in our afflictions if we let it in. It has been her experience that if we seek God in our difficulties, we will indeed find joy.

When she received her cancer diagnosis, she struggled a lot—especially being diagnosed with two different kinds of cancer within ten days. It has by far been the hardest thing she's ever gone through. The lack of control, with all the unknowns, has been soul-crushing. It has broken her in every possible way and more. It's easy to compare and wonder *why*, but she is trying to ask *what* instead—what is she able to learn, and what is she able to do for others and herself? Along the way, she has seen many tender mercies and flat-out miracles. It has been a sacred space—a space to grow and learn.

The more she has thought about this "test," the more she has wondered if it's a test at all or actually just an opportunity to turn to her Savior. A quote by Sister Amy A. Wright has helped her. She said, "I learned in a profound way that deliverance from our trials is different for each of us, and therefore our focus should be less about the *way* we are delivered and more about the Deliverer Himself. . . . When we submit to the will of the Lord, we will ultimately receive substantially more than that which we had desired."[1]

Afflictions aren't joyful, but because we have a loving Heavenly Father and the ability to return home to Him through our Savior, we can feel joy that our afflictions are temporary. And we will one day rejoice in the ultimate joy of being with Them again, without the pain. A wise bishop once told her that we all have to walk up mountains in our lives. If we have to do it anyway, why would we want to walk without God? She wants to walk up her mountains 100% with the Savior. As her cancer journey continues, she is working hard to not let her experiences *define* her but rather *refine* her as they make her who she is. God is good!

A few chapters later, in Alma 36, Alma testifies and teaches his son Helaman about his own conversion and how God delivered him. He said, "I do know that whosoever shall put their trust in God shall be supported in their trials, and their troubles, and their afflictions, and shall be lifted up at the last day" (Alma 36:3). And in verse 27, he said, "I have been supported under trials and troubles of every kind, yea, and in all manner of afflictions; yea, God has delivered me" (Alma 36:27)

This promise of deliverance in God's time is echoed throughout the Book of Mormon, starting in 1 Nephi (see verse 20).

President Eyring said, "I testify that by the Spirit of Christ and by the Holy Ghost, you may walk confidently in whatever difficulties will come. Because you are so valuable, some of your trials may be severe. You need never be discouraged or afraid. The way through difficulties has always been prepared for you, and you will find it if you exercise faith."[2]

Self-Reflection:
What are you doing to find joy in your afflictions?

54

PURE HAPPINESS

"And oh, what joy, and what marvelous light I did behold;
yea my soul was filled with joy as exceeding as was my pain."
(Alma 36:20)

ALMA IS GIVING HIS PERSONAL TESTIMONY ABOUT JESUS CHRIST TO his son Helaman. He talked about being a vile sinner drawing people away from God, and how a holy angel appeared to him, telling him he would be destroyed if he didn't repent. He was then struck dumb for three days and said of the experience, "I was tormented with the pains of hell; yea, I saw . . . that I had not kept his holy commandments" (Alma 36:13).

What does it mean to repent? A returned sister missionary shared her thoughts of this.

She used to have a negative view of repentance. She knew she needed to do it but felt that repenting would mean she had a mark on her record—as if Jesus Christ had a clipboard and was tallying all her faults. As she grew up, she realized how absurd it was to believe that a loving God would judge her without any mercy. She has come to realize what the Atonement of Jesus Christ truly means.

While Alma's soul was "harrowed up" by the memory of his many sins, he said, "Behold, I remembered also to have heard my father prophesy unto the people concerning the coming of one Jesus Christ, a son of God, to atone for the sins of the world" (Alma 36:17). She loves this! When he remembered, he cried out for mercy, and once he did, the pains of his sins were gone. From that moment on, Alma was a changed man and became a great prophet of the Lord. He tells us, "And oh, what joy, and what marvelous light I did behold; yea, my soul was filled with joy as exceeding as was my pain" (Alma 36:20).

To her, Alma is a wonderful example of true repentance and change.

President Joseph F. Smith once said, "True repentance is not only sorrow for sins and humble penitence and contrition before God, but it involves the necessity of turning away from them, a discontinuance of all evil practices and deeds, a thorough reformation of life, a vital change from evil to good, from vice to virtue, from darkness to light."[1]

During her first semester of college, she had a spiritual experience with this principle when the Spirit kept telling her to go meet with her bishop. She struggled to follow that prompting because she was afraid the bishop would judge her and she didn't want to face it. Then she heard Elder Bednar do a "Question & Answer" session with the young adults. He talked about resolving sin and recognizing what causes the Holy Ghost to withdraw. She realized what the Lord had been trying to tell her, and she knew she had to listen to the guidance of the Holy Ghost.

After she met with her bishop, she felt indescribable joy. A huge weight had been taken from her shoulders, and she felt the redeeming power of Jesus Christ envelop her. She learned what repentance felt like and why Satan was trying to keep her and everyone else from doing it. Repentance changes us. It is the way to access the Atonement of Jesus Christ. In that moment, she felt like Alma experiencing that pure happiness—the joy of repentance.

Self-Reflection:
Have you experienced an "Alma" moment?

55

SMALL AND SIMPLE

"Behold I say unto you, that by small and simple things are great things brought to pass. And by very small means the Lord . . . bringeth about the salvation of many souls." (Alma 37:6–7)

ALMA IS CONTINUING TO TEACH THE COMMANDMENTS TO HIS SON Helaman, preparing him to take the plates of Nephi, add to them, and keep them sacred like he has done. Alma tells Helaman, like those before, that "they are preserved for a wise purpose, which purpose is known unto God" (Alma 37:12). Alma also spoke with him concerning twenty-four gold plates that contained the history of the Jaredites—known to us as the book of Ether—which Helaman also needed to keep.

He tells Helaman that even though it may seem foolish to care so much about preserving the records, it is by "small and simple things" (Alma 37:6) that the Lord accomplishes His "great and eternal purposes" (Alma 37:7). He explains that this may confuse or bewilder those who are intelligent or learned, but small means bless and save many souls.

Small things can have a big impact. Like James taught in the New Testament, "Behold, we put bits in the horses' mouths, that they may obey us; and we turn about their whole body. Behold also the ships, which though they be so great, and are driven of fierce winds, yet they are turned about with a very small helm" (James 3:3–4).

Or consider a young boy of fourteen who had a question he couldn't answer, so he took it to God in prayer. It was early spring, in a quiet grove of trees, when his simple request began a turn of events that led to the coming forth of a sacred book of scripture that powerfully testifies how to gain peace in this life and eternal salvation in the world to come. A book that witnesses, like the Bible, of the ministry of the Savior Jesus Christ. A book that would eventually be translated into 115 languages so far, and which is the cornerstone of our church, The Church of Jesus Christ of Latter-day Saints—a Christian religion which that young boy, Joseph Smith, eventually restored based on the original church founded by Jesus Christ. And now we have over sixteen million members worldwide.

Through a small question and a simple prayer, God has changed the lives of millions of people.

God has also directed me in small ways, leading me to impactful changes and experiences.

Meeting my husband Trent began with a thought, which precipitated an action, which then led to more thoughts and more actions until we first met in person. Then our courtship began and unfolded with talking, interacting, spending time together, prayer, spiritual confirmation, and direction, culminating in sacred covenant-making in the house of the Lord.

Each manuscript I've written started with a feeling, a thought, or an idea, and then the first sentence. The entire process, however, included days, weeks, and months of progress through expanding ideas, research, contemplating, writing, re-writing, formal editing, review, publishing contracts, cover design, endorsements, line editing, marketing plans, advertising, printing, and delivery—until finally I held a completed book in my hands and saw it on store shelves.

There was a brother who had been less active for close to forty-five years. He was supportive of his wife and son's faithful activity in the Church, yet for his own reasons, he didn't participate. Then a simple change was made. He and his wife started reading one chapter of the Book of Mormon every day, and he began to transform. Others noticed a difference in his countenance and demeanor. His interest in the book soon expanded into reading more than one chapter a day, and he added heartfelt prayer. About six month later, he attended church. Eventually, after returning to regular activity, he received a calling and a few months later was ordained an elder. About a year later, he and his wife knelt across the altar in the temple and were sealed for time and all eternity.[1]

Small and simple things—choices and actions—can over time direct our life in big ways, either for good or for bad. As Elder Bednar taught:

> We can learn much about the nature and importance of this spiritual pattern from the technique of . . . dripping water onto the soil at very low rates. . . .
>
> The steady drips of water sink deep into the ground and provide a high moisture level in the soil wherein plants can flourish. In like manner, if you and I are focused and frequent in receiving consistent drops of spiritual nourishment, then gospel roots can sink deep into our soul, can become firmly established and grounded, and can produce extraordinary and delicious fruit.[2]

On the other hand, we must be careful to avoid small negative actions. As President Dallin H. Oaks said:

> Small and simple things can be negative and destructive to a person's salvation. . . .
>
> Those "seemingly insignificant" private decisions include how we use our time, what we view on television and the internet, what we read, the art and music with which we surround ourselves at work and home, what we seek for entertainment, and how we apply our commitment to be honest and truthful. Another seemingly small and simple thing is being civil and cheerful in our personal interactions. . . .
>
> Similarly, even small acts of disobedience or minor failures to follow righteous practices can draw us down toward an outcome we have been warned to avoid. . . .
>
> Like weak fibers that form a yarn [that aren't much on their own], then a strand, and finally a rope, these small things can become too strong to be broken. . . .

We must be aware that Satan will use small and simple things to lead us into despair and misery.[3]

> ### *Self-Reflection:*
> *What simple thing can you change in your life to help bring you closer to God?*

56

GIVE JESUS THE WHEEL

"Yea, and cry unto God for all thy support; yea, let all thy doings be unto the Lord, and whithersoever thou goest let it be in the Lord. . . . Counsel with the Lord in all thy doings, and he will direct thee for good." (Alma 37:36–37)

WE CONTINUE IN CHAPTER 37 WITH ALMA GIVING HIS SON HELAMAN parental counsel to pray always and keep his heart focused on the Savior, "and he will direct thee for good" (Alma 37:37).

That wise counsel applies to us today. When we counsel with the Lord through prayer, beginning in the morning of each day, He can continually direct us. Elder Bednar explains how this works:

Meaningful morning prayer is an important element in the spiritual creation of each day—and precedes the temporal creation or the actual execution of the day. . . .

There may be things in our character, in our behavior, or concerning our spiritual growth about which we need to counsel with Heavenly Father in morning prayer. After expressing appropriate thanks for blessings received, we plead for understanding, direction, and help to do the things we cannot do in our own strength alone. . . .

During the course of the day, we keep a prayer in our heart for continued assistance and guidance. . . .

At the end of our day, we kneel again and report back to our Father. . . . We repent and, with the assistance of the Spirit of the Lord, identify ways we can do and become better tomorrow. Thus our evening prayer builds upon and is a continuation of our morning prayer. And our evening prayer also is a preparation for meaningful morning prayer. . . .

[These prayers] and all the ones in between . . . are linked together. . . . This is in part how we fulfill the scriptural admonition to "pray always."[1]

Continuously "checking in" with the Lord through prayer keeps His guiding hand on us and brings reassurance and peace. In a recent sacrament meeting talk given by a new convert of only a few months, he mentioned that the word *peace* can be found more than 122 times in the Book of Mormon. The speaker related a significant contrast between the amount of peace he felt before and after his conversion and baptism, saying that the peace he now had in his life was much greater. He also presented a powerful visual analogy—an imaginary steering wheel in the back of his head. He stated that before he joined the Church, there were many other people and things that tried to control his steering wheel. He frankly admitted that this often sent him on a twisted and uneven course toward the cliffs. Since he has given the wheel to Jesus, letting all his comings and goings be in the Lord and trying to counsel with Him in everything, he has been driving on clear open roads, free of the confusion and turmoil he once felt.

Jesus is the way!

Self-Reflection:
Is there something in your life you need to let Jesus take charge of?

57

Poisoned by Degrees

"And it came to pass that Amalickiah caused that one of his servants should administer poison by degrees to Lehonti, that he died." (Alma 47:19)

In this section of the book of Alma, Alma has recently departed from Zarahemla, assumed to have passed on. It is the beginning of the nineteenth year of the reign of the judges, and Alma's son Helaman and his brethren went forth among the Nephites, teaching God's word to establish the Church again among all the land. They appointed priests and teachers in different cities to be over the churches, but some dissension arose (see Alma 45:18–24).

One of the leaders of the opposing groups was Amalickiah, "a large and a strong man . . . [who] was desirous to be a king" (Alma 46:3–4). He had followers who wanted him to be king as well, and many in the Church believed in his flattering words when he promised that if they supported him, he would make them rulers. His wickedness deceived the hearts of many people and led them to seek to destroy the Church. Eventually, due to the righteous opposition of his cause, led by Captain Moroni, Amalickiah took what followers he had left and departed into the wilderness.

When Amalickiah reached the land of Nephi, he "did stir up the Lamanites to anger against the people of Nephi, insomuch that the king of the Lamanites sent a proclamation throughout all his land . . . that they should gather themselves . . . to go to battle" (Alma 47:1). This caused a division among the people of the Lamanites. Many were afraid to displease their king but also afraid to go to battle and lose their lives. Amalickiah used this division to plot to overthrow the Lamanite king, Lehonti, so he could "dethrone him and take possession of the kingdom" (Alma 47:8). Amalickiah's plan unfolded as he set himself up in place to take over and then had the king murdered by poison, administered "by degrees" (Alma 47:19).

A sister heard the Savior's voice through this scripture story while struggling with a food addiction for many of her adult years. She gained weight gradually and didn't really notice until her clothes no longer fit. She was shocked when she saw a picture of herself and decided she needed to do something different. It wasn't just wanting to lose weight to be "skinny"—it was a sincere desire to feel better and be healthy. She realized her addiction to food was a form of abuse against the sacred gift Heavenly Father had given her—her body. She had been taking it for granted and had been an ungrateful steward.

She fasted and prayed for help.

She remembered a past conversation with a friend she served with at a Young Women's girls camp. The friend had told her she had given up flour and sugar because they were addictive. At the time, she thought her friend was crazy and that there was no way *she* could ever do that—flour and sugar were two of her very favorite things! But she was ready to make sacrifices to be healthier and show Heavenly Father she was grateful for her body.

At first, it was difficult for her to find other types of foods to eat that didn't contain these two ingredients. But then she got creative. She also found there were lots of other people doing the same thing. As she continued to cut flour and sugar out of her diet and add more unprocessed whole foods, she felt much better and was amazed at the results. Things in her life felt easier to manage as she lost weight and became healthier. She finally felt she was following the Word of Wisdom the way God had directed *her* to. She felt good following the personal spiritual direction she had received.

She had great success with these dietary changes for about a year and a half until the COVID-19 pandemic began. Then she started to slip a little here and there, slowly and subtly at first. Flour and sugar seemed to be everywhere—work, home, family members' and friends' houses—and she felt pressure to eat the things that contained them. It wasn't long before she was "enslaved" again.

She fasted and prayed again for strength and direction. This time it came from the Book of Mormon.

One morning, she was reading in the book of Alma. In chapter 47, she read about Amalickiah having one of his servants administer poison to King Lehonti by degrees until he died. It was so slow that he didn't even notice. It was so subtle that he didn't see it. He had no idea it was even happening. She realized she was just like Lehonti, only she was poisoning herself with unhealthy food, and she had done it by degrees.

Heavenly Father has given us so many blessings, like our bodies, and Satan tries to get us to misuse them. As a nurse, she sees a health-care system full of people who are sick and in pain as a result of what they choose to put in their mouths—things that look appealing and bring momentary comfort and pleasure but are ultimately detrimental to their health.

She has realized that Satan wants her to be addicted. He wants her to be in pain physically and spiritually. He doesn't have a body, and he wants her to abuse hers so she will be "miserable like unto himself" (2 Nephi 2:27).

Since this revelation, she views food and her body in a different way. As she has slowly gotten back to not eating flour or sugar, she has started to feel better. Her body is a temple. It takes hard work and sacrifice to keep temples beautiful inside and out, and the same is true for her body. She can't eat whatever she wants and expect there to be no negative consequences. She needs to put things in her mouth that will help her be healthy inside and out.

It is easier now that she can see Satan's tactics. She is grateful she can hear Heavenly Father through the Book of Mormon. She reads her scriptures daily and says a prayer before she starts, and there have been so many times He has spoken. She know He will continue to bless and guide her when she is in the right place, reading His word, and as she heeds His voice, she will "know the truth of all things" (Moroni 10:5).

Self-Reflection:
Do you pray before you read your scriptures?

58

ALWAYS PREPARED

"And now it came to pass that Moroni did not stop making preparations for war." (Alma 50:1)

IN THE PAST SEVERAL CHAPTERS, THE NEPHITES AND LAMANITES have been at war. The battles between them were intense, but their reasons for fighting were not the same.

The contrast was significant.

Captain Moroni was leading the Nephite people "to support their lands, and their houses, and their wives, and their children, that they might preserve them from the hands of their enemies; and also that they might preserve their rights and their privileges, yea, and also their liberty, that they might worship God according to their desires" (Alma 43:9). On the other hand, the intentions of the Lamanites (the descendants of Laman and Lemuel along with Nephite dissenters) were "to destroy their brethren, or to subject them and bring them into bondage that they might establish a kingdom unto themselves over all the land" (Alma 43:29).

Both sides had great loss of life, but throughout the battles, Moroni relied on the Lord, took counsel from Him, remained focused on the purpose, and did all he could to be prepared and to prepare his men. He remained steadfast in the belief that "God will support, and keep, and preserve us, so long as we are faithful unto him, and unto our faith, and unto our religion" (Alma 44:4).

After four years of being free from wars among themselves, contention against the Lamanites again arose. But the continued preparation and fortification of the Nephites surprised the Lamanites, and they did not succeed in their plan to gain power over the Nephites. Eventually, more than a thousand Lamanites were killed, without the Nephites losing even one, and the Lamanites again retreated.

Peace and prosperity returned among the Nephites, but as the twentieth year of the reign of the judges commenced, "Moroni did not stop making preparations for war" (Alma 50:1), preparing to defend his people against the Lamanites.

We might wonder why these chapters were included in Mormon's record, but aren't we *all* at war today? And like Moroni never letting his guard down in defending his people, we too must never let our guard down or stop preparing in defending ourselves against the adversary. The battle against good and evil is continuous, and the outcome of our war against Satan, "the father of all lies" (2 Nephi 2:18)—the war for our very souls—will affect us eternally.

Satan "knows he can't improve, he can't progress . . . [and] he will never have a brighter tomorrow. He is a miserable man bound by eternal limitations, and he wants [us] to be miserable too."[1] This means he is relentless in "his efforts to erode our personal spiritual foundation."[2] But we are stronger than he is, and we "were taught in the spirit world to prepare [us] for anything and everything [we] would encounter during this latter part of these latter days. That teaching endures within you!"[3]

We can be assured that when we feel opposition to something good we are trying to do, there is a reason. "Opposition to our cause testifies of its divinity. Would satanic powers combine against us if we were not posing a threat to such powers?"[4] The answer is simple: no!

Self-Reflection:
What are you doing to stay prepared against the adversary, even when things seem calm?

59

Offense Is a Choice

"The cause why they did not send more strength unto us, we knew not. . . . Therefore we did pour out our souls in prayer unto God, that he would strengthen us and deliver us. . . . Yea, and it came to pass that the Lord our God did visit us with assurances . . . [and] he did speak peace to our souls."
(Alma 58:9–11)

In chapter 56, Helaman sends an epistle to Captain Moroni updating him on what has gone on "in the borders of the land on the south by the west sea" (Alma 53:22). He let him know that two thousand of the young men Ammon brought down out of the land of Nephi had taken up their weapons of war and asked him to be their leader. He related the defense they gave to the army of Antipus, how brave the stripling warriors were, and how all two thousand of them were miraculously preserved by the Lord during the battles against the Lamanites.

As other battles in different areas occurred, Helaman and his men were weakened and began to run low on provisions and supplies. Helaman sent an embassy to the governor letting him know what they needed. Meanwhile, the Lamanites were fortifying themselves and their provisions, "resolving by stratagem to destroy [the Nephites]" (Alma 58:6).

Helaman and his men waited in these difficult circumstances for many months, "even until [they] were about to perish for the want of food" (Alma 58:7). Finally, they did receive food and an additional two thousand men "to contend with an enemy that was innumerable" (Alma 58:8). They didn't understand why no more support was sent. They "were grieved and also filled with fear" (Alma 58:9).

This turned them to God.

The account tells us, "The cause why they did not send more strength unto us, we knew not. . . . Therefore we did pour out our souls in prayer unto God, that he would strengthen us and deliver us. . . . Yea, and it came to pass that the Lord our God did visit us with assurances . . . [and] he did speak peace to our souls" (Alma 58:9–11).

In this stressful and confusing situation, with dire consequences, Helaman and his men received peace from God. He increased their faith, and they decided to hold on to hope that deliverance through Him would come. In the next verse, it says, "We did take courage with our small force which we had received, and were fixed with a determination to conquer our enemies, and to maintain our lands, and our possessions, and our wives, and our children, and the cause of our liberty. And thus we did go forth with all our might against the Lamanites, who were in the city of Manti" (Alma 58:12–13).

They turned their fear into faith, and instead of wallowing in anger and offense that their government didn't do more to come to their aid, they turned to the Lord. There was more to the story—they just didn't know it at that point.

Moroni didn't know the whole story either, and he ended up falsely accusing Pahoran (the chief judge and governor) for not sending Helaman and his men more help. Moroni did not mince words in his accusations. "Can you think to sit upon your thrones in a state of thoughtless stupor, while your enemies are spreading the work of death around you? Yea, while they are murdering thousands of your brethren?" (Alma 60:7). Moroni went on to call the government slothful, neglectful, idle, and possible traitors to their country. Moroni didn't know Pahoran had been exiled and the capital of Zarahemla taken over by the king-men.

Pahoran could have responded in like to Moroni's harsh words. Instead, he said, "In your epistle you have censured me, but it mattereth not; I am not angry. But do rejoice in the greatness of your heart. I, Pahoran do not seek for power, save only to retain my judgment-seat that I may preserve the rights and liberty of my people. My soul standeth fast in that liberty in the which God hath made us free" (Alma 61:9).

Pahoran didn't waver in who he was.

Helaman didn't lose faith.

When we don't know the "whole story" or are falsely accused, we have a choice—a choice whether or not to be offended. When I have struggled with this personally, it always goes better if I can give the other person the benefit of the doubt. So many things go on behind the scenes of another person's words or actions, and the backstory is rarely known in detail. And even when I have been hurt by others' rudeness or unkindness, I can still choose how I react.

"Brigham Young once said that he who takes offense when no offense was intended is a fool, and he who takes offense when offense *was* intended is usually a fool. It was then explained that there are two courses of action to follow when one is bitten by a rattlesnake. One may, in anger, fear, or vengefulness, pursue the creature and kill it. Or he may make full haste to get the venom out of his system. If we pursue the latter course we will likely survive, but if we attempt to follow the former, we may not be around long enough to finish it."[1]

Self-Reflection:
How will you choose to react the next time someone offends you?

PART X

THE BOOK OF HELAMAN
(ABOUT 52–1 BC)

*"The Book of Mormon has come forth
to remind us of the covenants of the
Lord, to the convincing of all 'that
Jesus is the Christ, the Eternal God,
manifesting himself unto all nations.'"*

—President Dallin H. Oaks[1]

60

PRIDE CAUSES WEAKNESS

"And they saw that they had become weak, like unto their brethren, the Lamanites, and that the Spirit of the Lord did no more preserve them; yea, it had withdrawn from them because the Spirit of the Lord doth not dwell in unholy temples."
(Helaman 4:24)

IN THE LAST CHAPTER OF THE BOOK OF ALMA, AT THE END OF THE thirty-sixth year of the reign of the judges, Captain Moroni dies, and Shiblon (one of the sons of Alma) takes over the plates for a short time. Many of the Nephites went northward, and some left on ships. Before Shiblon's death, he passed the plates on to Helaman, the son of Helaman. There were other Nephite dissenters who stirred up the Lamanites to anger, and Moronihah, the son of Captain Moroni, took over command of the armies and battled against them, driving them back to their own lands (see Alma 63).

The book of Helaman starts with contention over the chief judgment-seat after Pahoran's death. Three of his sons contended for the seat, and the people were divided as to who should get it. After Pahoran, the second son was chosen, but then a man named Kishkumen murdered him in disguise before quickly fleeing. Then Pacumeni was placed on the judgment-seat. A year later, the Lamanites attacked the city of Zarahemla and took possession of it, and Pacumeni was killed. Battles ensued between the Lamanites and the Nephites. Eventually, the Nephites conquered after much bloodshed and took possession of Zarahemla again (see Helaman 1).

Helaman, the son of Helaman, was appointed to "fill the judgment-seat, by the voice of the people" (Helaman 2:2). Meanwhile, Kishkumen remained hidden and made plans to destroy Helaman as well, joining forces with Gadianton. Gadianton was a robber who "was an expert in many words, also in his craft, to carry on the secret work of murder and of robbery; therefore he became the leader of the band of Kishkumen" (Helaman 2:4). At the end of chapter 2, a servant of Helaman thwarted Kishkumen's plan to murder Helaman and ended up stabbing Kishkumen in the heart. When Helaman tried to prosecute and execute the Gadianton robbers according to the law, they fled into hiding.

Contentions among the Nephites ebbed and flowed. During the times of peace, they multiplied, prospered, and were blessed "unto the baptizing and uniting to the church of God, many souls, yea, even tens of thousands" (Helaman 3:26).

When pride crept in because of great riches and prosperity, there began "the persecution of many of their brethren. Now this was a great evil, which did cause the more humble part the people to suffer great persecutions, and to wade through much affliction" (Helaman 3:34). In the fifty-third year of the reign of the judges, Helaman died, and his oldest son, Nephi, took over the judgment-seat and "did keep the commandments of God, and did walk in the ways of his father" (Helaman 3:37). In chapter 4, dissension and contention among the Nephites increased, as did their pride, and the strength of the Church dwindled.

As we read through these early chapters in Helaman, we see the repeated pattern of obedience and righteousness bringing blessings and prosperity, then pride and wickedness causing apostasy, suffering, and destruction. As I studied these chapters, the word *weak* in Helaman 4:24 stood out to me: "And they saw that they had become weak, like unto their brethren, the Lamanites, and that the Spirit of the Lord did no more preserve them; yea, it had withdrawn from them because the Spirit of the Lord doth not dwell in unholy temples."

When are the times in life we feel weak? What is the cause?

Trent and I discussed this together and had similar thoughts, recognizing we have felt weak when we have been fearful, angry, discouraged, prideful, sinning, or struggling with inadequacy. None of these feelings occur when we are close to the Spirit. In fact, they only occur when we are feeling the opposite—feeling our imperfect human state.

The answer to overcome all "weak" human frailties is to turn toward God and our Savior and repent. This creates change. As Elder Kevin S. Hamilton taught:

> One of Satan's greatest lies is that men and women cannot change. This untruth gets told and retold in many different ways as the world says that we simply cannot change—or worse yet, that we should not change. We are taught that our circumstances define us. We should "embrace who we really are," the world says, "and be authentic to our true selves." . . . Our real, true selves [are] sons and daughters of God with a divine nature and destiny.[1]

Also, the scriptures teach that we can be changed—"changed from [our] carnal and fallen state, to a state of righteousness, being redeemed . . . and thus [we] become new creatures" (Mosiah 27:25–26). In the New Testament, we read something similar: "Therefore if any man be in Christ, he is a new creature: old things are passed away; behold, all things are become new" (2 Corinthians 5:17)

A couple struggling with pride in their marriage had decided their relationship was hopeless and were in the final stages of preparing for divorce. As a last effort, they met with a religious counselor, as other secular counseling had had little effect.

The new counselor was frank with them. He recognized they had been caught up in worldly behaviors and attitudes, which taught that forcing, controlling, and commanding are the way to gain influence. The couple blamed one another for their problems and tried using intimidation and punishment to get their spouse to change, but it wasn't working. They had failed to apply gospel principles, which included focusing inward on their own behaviors and hearts.

After their first counseling visit, the couple attended the temple together. While they were in the celestial room, each of them asked in private prayer to know what they as individuals had been doing wrong to create the wide division in their marriage. God poured out his Spirit upon them in the form of answers. The personal revelation they each received humbled and softened their hearts. They were grateful for His grace and mercy.

Over time, they made progress as they shifted the blame away from each other and toward their own need for repentance and change. They also recognized important things they had stopped doing daily because of their pride—regular prayer and scripture study. Their hearts were broken as they realized that their actions and preoccupation with their own self-interests were destroying any possibility for oneness. Eventually, this couple was able to regain the love they had lost.[2]

Pride and lust for riches is addressed several times throughout the Book of Mormon, but in the book of Helaman, which is only sixteen chapters long, it seems to be the sin that is condemned the most. For example, pride and lust for riches were listed first in Helaman 4:12 as the reasons why the Nephites were losing the war. The people were chastised for these sins again in Helaman 7:21 when Nephi gave his garden speech from a tower. And in Helaman 13, Samuel the Lamanite strongly expounded on how seeking wealth leads to other sins and how being prideful leads people to justify their sins.

Pride also seems often to have many faces: faultfinding, gossiping, envying, being unforgiving, jealousy, selfishness, contention, defensiveness, rebelliousness, hard-heartedness, being judgmental, comparing yourself to others, living beyond our means, coveting, vainness, smugness, immodesty, being unrepentant, taking offense easily, being competitive, withholding gratitude, disobedience, self-pity, self-gratification, abuse, grudge-holding, rationalization, and more.[3]

Not all of our weaknesses or struggles with pride look the same. But our Savior's "strengthening, enabling grace gives us power to overcome *all* obstacles, *all* challenges, and *all* weaknesses as we seek to change."[1]

Self-Reflection:
What is one weak thing in yourself you can pray for help to overcome?

61

REMOVING CLOUDS OF DARKNESS

"And it came to pass that the Lamanites said unto him: What shall we do that this cloud of darkness may be removed from overshadowing us?" (Helaman 5:40)

IN THIS CHAPTER, NEPHI GIVES UP THE JUDGMENT-SEAT BECAUSE HE became "weary" (Helaman 5:4) of the iniquity of the Nephites, and he and his brother Lehi wanted to preach the word of God full time. They reflected and reiterated the words their father Helaman had taught them, wanting to teach them among the people. They did so with "great power, insomuch that they did confound many of those dissenters . . . insomuch that they came forth and did confess their sins and were baptized unto repentance" (Helaman 5:17). They also had great success among the Lamanites, baptizing eight thousand of them in the land of Zarahemla.

Next they went to the land of Nephi, where they were taken by an army of Lamanites and cast into prison. While they were captive, they went many days without food, and when they were about to be killed, they were encircled by fire. Their captors were not able to touch them, yet Nephi and Lehi were not burned. This gave them courage, and they began to testify of God, knowing He was with them. The earth shook, and they were overshadowed with a cloud of darkness.

Then the people heard a voice, "not a voice of thunder, neither a voice of a great tumultuous noise, but behold it was a still voice of perfect mildness, as if it had been a whisper, and it did pierce even to the very soul" (Helaman 5:30). This voice told their captors to repent. The Lamanites were afraid, but they could not flee because they were overshadowed by a "cloud of darkness."

A sister shared the following experience related to this story.

Often she has found herself consumed by the heaviness of situations that people find themselves in—the suffering, the trials, and the pain of so many people, including children. This leaves her feeling conflicted. We are told to "mourn with those that mourn" (Mosiah 18:9), but we also hear the phrase "let go and let God." It feels like such a fine line. What can you do when you feel enveloped by darkness?

In this story in Helaman, when the Lamanites asked what they could do to have the cloud of darkness removed from them, they were answered by a Nephite who was among them—a man named Aminadab who had once been a member of the Church but had left. Through the cloud of darkness, this man was able to see that Nephi and Lehi had been conversing with angels. He told the other Lamanites (a group of about three hundred) that they needed to repent, cry unto the voice they had heard, and have faith in Christ.

In Helaman 5:49, it says that the people were told to "go forth and marvel not, neither should they doubt." To her, this felt like an odd request. As humans, we see fire and assume it'll burn whatever is in its way, but Nephi and Lehi weren't touched. Seeing people converse with angels isn't a common occurrence either. But to God, these things are not uncommon, and the people were told not to doubt because with God it was possible.

She sometimes thinks that not having "opposition in all things" (2 Nephi 2:11) would be preferable. If everything was good, we might not know we have it good since we don't know the bad, but still, everything would be good! Yet there's a flip side. If everything was all bad, and there was no hope for things ever getting better, and the bad just kept coming, how awful would that be?

This makes her feel an even deeper gratitude for her Savior. Through facing trials with Him, she receives hope that the light of the sunrise on the horizon will come, dispelling the dreary night. She knows God can make some pretty beautiful things out of some really dark situations—she has seen it and lived it. We don't need to doubt or marvel because "with God all things are possible" (Matthew 19:26). And if we record those beautiful experiences, like the writers of the Book of Mormon did, we will remember them in times of future questioning.

In order to not be held back by "clouds of darkness," we must seek and embrace the light. Spiritually, "our growth is determined by how we follow the Son—the Son of God—and allow His light to be the controlling force."[1]

> **Self-Reflection:**
> *What cloud of darkness can the Savior remove for you?*

62

Prophets Testify

"Behold now, I do not say that these things shall be, of myself,
because it is not of myself that I know these things; but behold, I
know that these things are true because the Lord God has made
them known unto me, therefore I testify that they shall be."
(Helaman 7:29)

NEPHI RETURNED TO THE LAND OF ZARAHEMLA IN THE SIXTY-NINTH year of the reign of the judges after preaching and prophesying in the land northward. He had been rejected and had seen much wickedness, the influence of the Gadianton robbers, the condemnation of the righteous, and the wicked going unpunished. "His heart was swollen with sorrow within his breast; and he did exclaim in the agony of his soul" (Helaman 7:6), wishing he could have been living in the days of his forefathers when the people were firm in keeping the commandments in the promised land.

He poured his soul out to God on a tower in his garden, and "men passing by" (Helaman 7:11) saw him. They ran and told others, and soon a multitude gathered around him, wondering why he was mourning so greatly. Nephi saw them and started to testify and share what was in his heart. The Spirit guided his words as God "made them known" (Helaman 7:29) unto him. Some of the listeners grew angry as he reviled the corruptness of their laws, speaking clearly of their works of darkness. Contentions among them increased, but "if he had not been a prophet he could not have testified concerning these things" (Helaman 8:9).

This scripture account reconfirmed to me that prophets know through the power of revelation exactly what God needs the people to hear, and they teach us from a place of love even when they must use bold words. Nephi was not in a good or happy place. He was full of "exceeding sorrow" and anguish over the sins and iniquities of his people. Even though God had chosen him to lead, he was still one of them, and his heart ached for his people.

Our prophets today come from the same place. They are one of us but have been called to lead, and sometimes that leading involves testifying boldly of things that may not be easy to hear when it involves repentance and change. But when we listen with humility and meekness to their counsel, we can receive our own confirmation through the Spirit regarding the truth of their words and what we need to do differently to grow closer to God.

Many times as I've listened to the prophet speak, especially during general conference, I've received personal revelation and direction about something I've been struggling with. More than once, I felt certain he wrote his talk just for me. However, not everything the prophet asks us to do is easy. President Eyring shares this counsel:

> The failure to take prophetic counsel lessens our power to take inspired counsel in the future. The best time to have decided to help Noah build the ark was the first time he asked. Each time he asked after that, each failure to respond would have lessened sensitivity to the Spirit. And so each time his request would have seemed more foolish, until the rain came. And then it was too late.
>
> Every time in my life when I have chosen to delay following inspired counsel or decided that I was an exception, I came to know that I had put myself in harm's way. Every time that I have listened to the counsel of prophets, felt it confirmed in prayer, and then followed it, I have found that I moved toward safety. Along the path, I have found that the way had been prepared for me and the rough places made smooth. God led me to safety along a path

which was prepared with loving care, sometimes prepared long before.[1]

Another wise Church leader said this: "Let us remember . . . that the further out of line or out of tune we ourselves are, the more we are inclined to look for error or weaknesses in others and to try to rationalize and justify our own faults rather than to try to improve ourselves. Almost invariably, we find that the greatest criticism of Church leaders and doctrine comes from those who are not doing their full duty, following the leaders, or living according to the teachings of the gospel."[2]

Helaman and other prophets in the Book of Mormon teach us many important truths, including that blessings come from heeding their words and that there is danger in rejecting them. "For behold, the Spirit of the Lord ceaseth soon to strive with them; for behold, they have rejected the prophets" (1 Nephi 7:14). This same truth applies to us today. When our ears are closed to things of the Spirit, "[we] will not understand the words which are spoken, according to their truth" (Alma 10:25).

Ultimately, all the prophets collectively taught the most important truth: "We talk of Christ, we rejoice in Christ, we prophesy of Christ, and we write according to our prophecies" (2 Nephi 25:26), and we can only be saved "through the merits, and mercy, and grace of the Holy Messiah" (2 Nephi 2:8).

Self-Reflection:
What is your commitment level to following the prophet?

63

REVELATION THROUGH PONDERING

*"Nephi went his way towards his own house, pondering
upon the things which the Lord had shown unto him. As he
was thus pondering—being much cast down because of the
wickedness of the Nephites . . . behold a voice came unto him."*
(Helaman 10:2–3)

NEPHI CONTINUES TO STRUGGLE OVER THE DIVISION OF THE
Nephites, some believing his words, and others—especially those
whose "secret works of darkness" (Helaman 8:4) he had called out—
sought to destroy him and "question him in divers ways that they
might cross him, that they might accuse him to death" (Helaman
9:19).

After the people "divided hither and thither and went their ways,
leaving Nephi alone . . . Nephi went his way towards his own house,
pondering upon the things which the Lord had shown unto him"
(Helaman 10:1–2). As he pondered and contemplated all that had
transpired, "being much cast down because of the wickedness of the
Nephites" (Helaman 10:3), the Lord spoke to him. He received personal revelation, comfort, and direction. He was told, "Blessed art

thou Nephi, for those things which thou hast done; for I have beheld how thou hast with unwearyingness declared the words which I have given unto thee, unto this people. And thou has not feared them, and thou hast not sought thine own life, but hast sought my will, and to keep my commandments" (Helaman 10:4).

When we are "cast down," anxious, or weary, we too can ponder, reflect, and receive our own revelation from the Lord for help in how to move forward—just like Nephi did.

When I have struggled or felt anxious personally, I always have two choices. I can wallow in the feelings of discouragement, anxiety, or sadness, feeling frantic and bereft—and when I do this, those feeling multiply, get worse, and often affect others around me, creating a more negative environment. Or I can slow my troubled mind down, think more logically than emotionally, pray, and turn to God and ask Him for assistance, either by helping me find the solution or strengthening me to endure.

I can remember an experience I had when a bird flew into my home through an open back door while I was doing some spring cleaning. How frantic it was as it flew from one side of the room to the other, trying more than once to exit through a solid window pane of glass, not understanding how useless the efforts of its fluttering wings were. With some guidance and direction, I was finally able to help it go back through the open door—to freedom. I can only image the relief that little bird must have finally felt.

How often are we like that little bird, fluttering our wings in panic at our troubled thoughts, whose outside view of relief is right in front of us but just beyond our grasp. Slowing down, breathing, letting our emotions settle, reading our scriptures, pondering them, and praying—all these things lead us to answers, direction, and revelation. They lead us to God and to freedom.

A sister shared the following:

One day at work, I started feeling frustrated—every way I tried to approach the project felt wrong. After struggling for a while, [a spiritual] impression came: *"I care about this project too, you know. Why don't you ask Me about it?"* I immediately stopped working to say a prayer and ask for guidance, which was mercifully given.

As I've reflected on that experience, I've come to realize that the impression could be applied to any aspect of my life. "I care about Church history. Why don't you ask Me?" "I care about what you study in college. Why don't you ask Me?" "I care about Church policies and procedures. Why don't you ask Me?"[1]

Elder Bednar said, "Sometimes the spirit of revelation will operate immediately and intensely, other times subtly and gradually, and often so delicately you may not even consciously recognize it. But regardless of the pattern whereby this blessing is received, the light it provides will illuminate and enlarge your soul [and] enlighten your understanding."[2]

Self-Reflection:
What will you do the next time you feel "cast down"?

64

MERCY, HOPE, LOVE

"But if ye will repent and return unto the Lord your God I will turn away mine anger, saith the Lord; yea, thus saith the Lord, blessed are they who will repent and turn unto me."
(Helaman 13:11)

IN THE EIGHTY-SIXTH YEAR OF THE REIGN OF THE JUDGES, ANOTHER prophet, Samuel the Lamanite, came into the land of Zarahemla to preach and warn the Nephites as directed by the Lord. He was cast out, but the Lord admonished him to return and "prophesy unto the people whatsoever things should come into his heart" (Helaman 13:3). Since they wouldn't let Samuel reenter the city, he preached on top of a wall, warning them that heavy destruction awaited them unless they repented and turned with faith to the Lord Jesus Christ who was coming into the world to "suffer many things and be slain for his people" (Helaman 13:6).

In these verses, we can see that despite the Lord's "fierce anger" (Helaman 13:10) over their sins and wickedness, there was still a way out. Samuel told them, and it applies to us too, that "if ye will repent and return unto the Lord your God I will turn away mine anger . . . yea, thus saith the Lord, blessed are they who will repent and turn unto me" (Helaman 13:11).

I love that our God is a God of mercy.

He is a God of second chances.

He is a God of hope.

He is a God of love.

I think about the woman in the New Testament whose story is related in the Gospel of John. It was early in the morning. I can imagine the light of a new day brightening the sky above the temple, a place where many sought solace, comfort, and spiritual communion. Jesus was teaching. I'm sure His listeners might have even been engrossed in a story, His words creating feelings of new hope and awe, and then there was a jarring disruption. I expect that the woman, being suddenly thrust before Him, was distraught and ashamed, her eyes darting and downcast, as the scribes and Pharisees cast their judgment, rehearsing her sins aloud for everyone to hear.

"Master, this woman was taken in adultery, in the very act. Moses in the law commanded us, that such should be stoned: but what sayest thou?" (John 8:4–5).

Jesus stayed calm, and He reminded them that if any in the crowd were without sin, they could cast the first stone. One by one, they all left until He was alone with her. And in His mercy, He did not condemn her or her sin. He simply said, "Go, and sin no more" (John 8:11). I'm sure her heart must have felt lightened and her burden of shame must have lifted—because He had given her a second chance.

We can be assured that "whosoever repenteth shall find mercy; and he that findeth mercy and endureth to the end the same shall be saved" (Alma 32:13).

Clinging to hope in our God, strengthened by faith in His unconditional love for us, can anchor our soul. Hope helps us improve when we are weak, and small but steady correct daily choices will help us change. Repentance is not something we do just once—it is a process. And "we know that it is by grace that we are saved, after all we can do" (2 Nephi 25:23).

A young man shared the following story.

At age fifteen, he wasn't making the best decisions. He often hung out with the wrong crowd and was surrounded by many temptations, some of which he gave in to. At first they seemed like small things, but before long he was in a dark place, hiding things from his family and feeling alone. He wasn't sure where to turn or if God even loved him.

One day, when things seemed particularly hard, he had the thought that he should start reading the Book of Mormon. As he began to study it, he felt something warm in his heart, and each page seemed to tell him he could change with the Savior's help. This gave him the courage to talk with his mom about decisions he had been making and things he had been doing. He expected her to be angry, but instead she told him how much she loved him. During their conversation, he felt God's love for the first time.

As he continued to read the scriptures and pray, he found the courage to speak with his bishop and start the repentance process. During that meeting, he felt the love of the Savior and Heavenly Father lift the burden of shame off his shoulders. Going through this experience taught him that repentance truly is a gift of love from Them, and he learned that hearts can be changed when intentions are sincere.[1]

Self-Reflection:
When have you felt God's mercy, hope, and love?

PART XI

THE BOOK OF THIRD NEPHI
(ABOUT 1 BC—AD 34–35)

"As you use your agency to carve out time every day to draw close to God's voice, especially in the Book of Mormon, over time His voice will become clearer and more familiar to you."

—Sister Michelle D. Craig[1]

65

NOT IN VAIN

*"But behold, they did watch steadfastly for that day and that
night and that day which should be as one day as if there were
no night, that they might know if their faith had not been in
vain." (3 Nephi 1:8)*

Six hundred years had passed since Lehi and his family left
Jerusalem, and Nephi, the grandson of Helaman and the son of
Nephi, was now keeping the records on the brass plates. Prophecies,
signs, and miracles were being fulfilled, but some argued "the time
was past for the words to be fulfilled, which were spoken by Samuel,
the Lamanite" (3 Nephi 1:5).

Those who doubted made a "great uproar" (3 Nephi 1:7) against
their brethren who were trying to remain faithful in the promises
Samuel made about the coming birth of the Savior. These believers
"did watch steadfastly for that day and that night and that day . . .
that they might know if their faith had not been in vain" (3 Nephi
1:8).

Samuel had prophesied there would be a sign:

For five years more cometh, and behold, then cometh the Son of
God to redeem all those who shall believe on his name. . . . For

a sign at the time of his coming . . . there shall be great lights in heaven, insomuch that in the night before he cometh there shall be no darkness, insomuch that it shall appear unto man as if it was day. Therefore, there shall be one day and a night and a day, as if it were one day and there were no night . . . and it shall be the night before he is born. (Helaman 14:2–4)

The doubters threatened "that all those who believed in those traditions should be put to death except the sign should come to pass" (3 Nephi 1:9). Nephi's "heart was exceedingly sorrowful" as he saw this wickedness of some of his people as the believers tried to hold on to their faith that the sign would still come. He "cried mightily to his God in behalf of his people, yea, those who were about to be destroyed because of their faith in the tradition of their fathers" (3 Nephi 1:10–11).

Do we ever have faith and then stumble while we wait for something to come to pass? Trent and I have experienced this personally when what we pray for, hope, and need seems far away. We've learned that sometimes it's darkest before the storm breaks. But in God's perfect timing, the sun returns, everything falls into place, and we are reminded—again—that He was there all along, that He had a plan, and that His words will all be fulfilled.

When I was desperately ready to move on in my life during my difficult divorce, my life felt like it was in limbo. I was in a temporary living situation, waiting to buy a house and start over somewhere new in a place not filled with painful memories and reminders. My finances and job were aligned to make the purchase, but I was unable to proceed with securing a loan until my divorce was finalized. Because my estranged husband wasn't ready to sign the legal papers we had drawn up, I was unable to do anything else except wait until he *was* ready.

As the weeks and months passed, I became more and more discouraged by the situation and my lack of control over it. Then I was given a tight deadline to move out of where I was renting at the time, and my anxiety greatly increased. This affected my ability to sleep and eat normally. Even though I prayed often for comfort and help, studied my scriptures, and faithfully attended my church meetings, I wondered where God was in this desire.

Every time I looked for a more permanent living arrangement that involved signing a lease to rent, I felt unsettled and confused. Finally, I sought a priesthood blessing. In that blessing, I was reminded that God was mindful of my situation, He did have a plan, and I needed to trust Him. Less than two weeks later, the divorce papers were signed. Within that same week, I found a house and made an offer that was accepted. Thirty days later, I closed on the house and moved in, within just a few days of the deadline to be out of the place I had been renting.

Even though my faith felt shaky, it "had not been in vain"—and God completely provided for me. My trust in Him through this experience was increased, as was my gratitude for His patience with me while I learned what I needed to.

God also came through for the people of Nephi—those that believed—and the doubters were proven wrong when the Lord told Nephi, "Be of good cheer; for behold, the time is as hand, and on this night shall the sign be given, and on the morrow I come into the world, to show unto the world that I will fulfil all that I have caused to be spoken by the mouth of my holy prophets" (3 Nephi 1:13).

Later that night, the night before Christ's birth, "at the going down of the sun there was no darkness; and the people began to be astonished because there was no darkness when the night came. . . . And it came to pass that the sun did rise in the morning again, according to its proper order; and they knew that it was the day that the Lord should be born. . . . And it had come to pass, yea, all things, every whit, according to the words of the prophets" (3 Nephi 1:15, 19–20).

President Nelson reminds us, "The mountains in our lives do not always move how or when we would like. But our faith will *always* propel us forward. . . . The Savior is never closer to you than when you are facing or climbing a mountain with faith. . . . Central to that faith is trusting His will and timetable."[1]

Self-Reflection:
What can you do today to strengthen your faith for tomorrow?

66

THE LIGHT OF THE WORLD

"Behold, I am Jesus Christ. . . . I am the light and the life of the world." (3 Nephi 11:10–11)

ABOUT THIRTY-FOUR YEARS AFTER THE NEPHITES WERE GIVEN THE sign that Christ had been born, "there arose a great storm, such an one as never had been known in all the land" (3 Nephi 8:5). It lasted for about three hours. The horrific storm included a great and terrible tempest, severe thunder, sharp lightnings, whirlwinds, and earthquakes. Cities were burned and sunk—some into the depths of the sea. There were many deaths. When the storm subsided, a thick darkness covered the deformed land, and for the next three days, there was no light seen anywhere.

In the darkness a voice started to speak—a voice from the heavens that was heard throughout the entire land. It was the voice of Jesus Christ, "the voice of the very person who had been mocked and ridiculed and rejected by the wicked! It was the voice of Him whom the prophets proclaimed and for whom they were stoned and killed! It was the voice of the Master!"[1]

He told them that He caused what they had just endured, and that those whose lives He had spared—theirs—were spared because they were not as wicked as those who had perished. And then with compassion He said, "Will ye not now return unto me, and repent of your sins, and be converted, that I may heal you? . . . Behold, mine arm of mercy is extended towards you, and whosoever will come, him will I receive" (3 Nephi 9:13–14).

He told them they should offer Him their "broken heart and contrite spirit" and that He would "baptize them with fire and with the Holy Ghost," (3 Nephi 9:20). He talked about repentance, and he said He had come to save the world from sin. After that, there was silence for many hours before He spoke again.

Once three days had passed, the darkness left and the earth quieted. "The wailing of the people who were spared alive did cease; and their mourning was turned into joy, and their lamentations into the praise and thanksgiving unto the Lord Jesus Christ, their Redeemer" (3 Nephi 10:10).

I try to imagine what I would have felt if I had been there. I'm sure there was great fear witnessing the terrible destruction, death, and extreme elements of the storm. I would think that those who didn't perish were terrified that they might. It had to have been a life-changing event on many levels, and being caught in unrelenting darkness must have only heightened their alarm. When I read about them hearing the voice of Jesus Christ, listening to Him say He was responsible for the major upheaval in their land, and then hearing His offers of healing and mercy if they would come to him, I'm sure they must have felt glimmers of hope and relief.

The Father's voice then introduced Him: "Behold my Beloved Son . . . in whom I have glorified my name—hear ye him" (3 Nephi 11:7). When He appeared, "descending out of heaven" (3 Nephi 11:8), the whole multitude fell to the earth—a group of about 2,500 men, women, and children. They thought He was an angel, but then they heard His voice, saying, "I am Jesus Christ, whom the prophets testified shall come into the world. And behold, I am the light and the life of the world" (3 Nephi 11:10–11).

They were then able to physically see Him, touch Him one by one, and be taught by Him. What an amazing thing they witnessed and felt! They came to know personally the reality of His resurrection, and "they did cry out with one accord, saying: Hosanna! Blessed be the name of the Most High God! And they did fall down at the feet of Jesus, and did worship him" (3 Nephi 11:16–17).

While we may not experience the exact same kind of destruction the people of Nephi did at that time, we have other kinds of "destruction" we face in our own lives—destruction that comes from many sources. His healing, His mercy, and His light can save us, just like it saved the people of Nephi, when we repent and turn to Him.

Trent and I have felt His healing when He has soothed our broken hearts, filling us with peace and comfort after receiving painful news about a loved one's medical diagnosis. We have felt His mercy when He has helped us overcome our weaknesses through the power of His Atonement and has reassured us that His grace is always there to catch us when we fall. We have felt His light when He has given us courage to press forward when the way has felt dark, uncertain, and troubled while facing heartache with some of our children. The list goes on and on.

Sister Sharon Eubank shared the following:

One night this past February, my office remained exceptionally dim as the sun went down. As I looked out the window, the temple was dark. The lights had not turned on. I felt suddenly somber. I couldn't see the temple spires I had glimpsed every evening for years.

Seeing darkness where I expected to see light reminded me that one of the fundamental needs we have in order to grow is to stay connected to our source of light—Jesus Christ. He is the source of our power, the Light and Life of the World. Without a strong connection to Him, we begin to spiritually die. Knowing that, Satan tries to exploit the worldly pressures we all face. He works to dim our light, short-circuit the connection, cut off the power supply, leaving us alone in the dark.[2]

How do we keep our connection to the light and power of Jesus Christ strong and keep the darkness of Satan away?

Our prophet, President Nelson, said, "The key is to make and keep sacred covenants."[3] And then we need to stay on the covenant path. We need to keep going even when it's hard, even when we have questions, and even when our faith feels small, and we need to pray for direction and strength. The scriptures promise, "The Lord hath heard the prayers of his people . . . [and] the prayers of his servants [will] be answered according to their faith" (Mosiah 27:14).

Self-Reflection:
How has the light of Christ touched you recently? Write about it in your journal.

67

CONTENTION: NOT OF HIM

"For verily, verily I say unto you, he that hath the spirit of contention is not of me, but is of the devil. But this is my doctrine, that such things should be done away with."
(3 Nephi 11:29–30)

AFTER JESUS CHRIST GAVE NEPHI AND THE OTHER DISCIPLES THE authority to baptize in His name, He told them, "The Father, and the Son, and the Holy Ghost are one; and I am in the Father, and the Father in me, and the Father and I are one" (3 Nephi 11:27). Then He went on to teach that after being baptized, there should not be any more disputations among them as in the past. This is because the spirit of contention is not of Him—it is of the devil, the father of contention.

Christ's explanation of the relationship that exists among the Godhead is a powerful example of unity and being one in purpose. President George Q. Cannon expressed, "Now can you conceive of a oneness more close, more complete than the oneness that exists between the Father and the Son? It is impossible for the human mind to get the faintest idea of any difference of opinion, or expression, or action between the Father and the Son."[1]

Contention—arguing, conflict, angry contesting, or strife—drives away peace. President Benson described it as "another face of pride,"[2] and we know it comes from Satan, not from God. "Yea, [Satan] did go about spreading rumors and contentions upon all the face of the land, that he might harden the hearts of the people against that which was good" (Helaman 16:22). When we give in to contention, in any form, the Spirit leaves. Without the Spirit, it is much harder to follow Christ in our thoughts, actions, and deeds. Contention can range "from a hostile spoken word to worldwide conflicts."[2]

The Book of Mormon teaches us how to counteract contention. "There was no contention in the land, because of the love of God which did dwell in the hearts of the people" (4 Nephi 1:15).

Having and sharing the love of God should be our goal. And when contention arises suddenly—as it often does, especially in relationships—the more quickly we recognize it in ourselves and make corrections, the faster we can restore peace and feel love.

On one occasion, it was dinnertime and my family was gathered around the table, hungry and ready to eat. The feeling in the dining room was not relaxed or carefree—it was tense. One of my children had been struggling in his interactions with other members of the family, and cross words had been spoken. That night, it was his turn to pray.

He was called on by name. Everyone else sat silently and waited. Despite his sour mood, he didn't protest—he folded his arms and started to bow his head. Suddenly, he dropped his arms, looked up, and firmly said, "I can't."

Four pairs of startled eyes focused on his.

He went on. "I don't feel the Spirit right now." He released a breath. "I need to get clear first."

He started by apologizing to his younger sister, then continued until he had addressed everyone at the table, one by one. Some he talked to longer than others, but when he finished, the feeling in our home had changed. The tension had dissipated.

"I'm ready now," he announced, then bowed his head once more. During his prayer, he thanked Heavenly Father for each of us, for his many blessings, and for the food we were about to eat. He also prayed that there would be no more contention in our home and that we would feel love. His words rang out warm and sincere.

The Spirit filled my heart in great abundance. I could see that the rest of the family felt it too. Unity was reinstated through my son's prayer, and his example taught us all.

Every time I have chosen to be patient and calm when someone upsets or offends me, I am much better able to handle the situation with grace, understanding, and love, and the issue gets resolved quickly.

Every time I have chosen the opposite—to be impatient, critical, or easily offended in relationships with others—negative feelings escalate and spread and the issue grows, often causing damage that isn't easily fixed.

I have learned that I absolutely prefer the former, and I am striving continually to eliminate the latter.

President Nelson gives perfect counsel on this:

> None of us can control nations or the actions of others or even members of our own families. But we can control ourselves. My call today, dear brothers and sisters, is to end conflicts that are raging in your heart, your home, and your life. Bury any and all inclinations to hurt others—whether those inclinations be a temper, a sharp tongue, or a resentment for someone who has hurt you. . . .
>
> We are followers of the Prince of Peace. Now more than ever, we need the peace only He can bring. . . .
>
> Exercise the humility, courage, and strength required both to forgive and to seek forgiveness. . . .
>
> As you do so, I promise personal peace.[3]

Self-Reflection:
What's one thing you can work on to reduce contention in your relationships?

68

THE LIGHT OF EXAMPLE

*"Therefore let your light so shine before this people, that they
may see your good works and glorify your Father who is in
heaven." (3 Nephi 12:16)*

JUST LIKE JESUS CHRIST TAUGHT HIS DISCIPLES AND A LARGE CROWD
of listeners during the Sermon on the Mount in Galilee in the Eastern
Hemisphere, he teaches a similar discourse to the people of Nephi
gathered by the temple in Bountiful in the Western Hemisphere. He
tells them to follow the twelve disciples He chose from among them
to minister and serve, and He says they would be "blessed" as they
followed His teachings and did certain things that pointed to Him
as the way.

The higher law He taught them replaced the law of Moses they
had been living under. "Marvel not that I said unto you that old things
had passed away, and that all things had become new. Behold, I say
unto you that the law is fulfilled that was given unto Moses. Behold, I
am he that gave the law . . . for I have come to fulfil the law; therefore
it hath an end" (3 Nephi 15:3–5).

Like His disciples and followers in the New Testament, Christ
also called the Nephites to be the "salt of the earth" and the "light of
this people" (3 Nephi 12:13–14). He then taught them to take that

"light" and shine it as an example before others, showing their "good works" to glorify Heavenly Father (3 Nephi 12:16).

As modern-day disciples of Jesus Christ, we are called to do the same.

The power of example can be far-reaching, creating rippling effects similar to a smooth pebble breaking the glassy surface of a pond, and often those setting an example don't even realize how important the effects of that example are—for good or for bad.

A brother who served in the Ecuadorian army after graduating from high school used some of his limited daily free time to study the Book of Mormon. When he came across this scripture about "[letting] your light so shine," he prayerfully asked for help applying it personally. As the only Latter-day Saint in his company of 104 young men, he stood out and sometimes was made fun of, but he stayed true to his standards and beliefs.

One day, his company discovered that the feed of one of the soldiers' automatic rifles was missing. In Ecuador, stealing something like this was considered a serious crime against the government and punishable by jail time. The entire company searched for it for three days without success. When the captain of the company decided all personal footlockers needed to be searched, the young man was astonished when it was found in his. He had no idea how it had gotten there.

The captain called him over and quietly asked for an explanation while many members of the company looked on. All he could say was he didn't know. The captain looked at him and said, "I know what your conduct has been all this time, and I know you didn't do it." Another officer nearby agreed. One by one, the other officers came up to him and also offered their support at his innocence.

Until that moment, he hadn't fully realized the blessing of obedience or the power of example. Tears began to run down his cheeks as he recognized the protecting power of the Savior. He knew that *He* was at his side. Because of this experience, the verse in 3 Nephi that had impressed him earlier will always be engraved on his mind. He is grateful the Book of Mormon taught him to be a light and an example.

A few days later, one of his friends in the company told him he had met with two missionaries and was going to be baptized the following week. His happiness was complete as he saw him join the Church.[1]

When Corianton, one of Alma's sons, followed after the harlot Isabel, his choices and example had far-reaching negative effects. Alma reproved Corianton's grievous behavior and said, "Behold, O my son, how great iniquity ye brought upon the Zoramites; for when they saw your conduct they would not believe my words" (Alma 39:11). Corianton's actions had the potential to lead away many people to destruction, but he responded to his father's inspired counsel, repented, and went on to be a missionary.

Example is powerful.

"Life is perfect for none of us, and at times the challenges and difficulties we face may become overwhelming, causing our light to dim. However, with help from our Heavenly Father, coupled with support from others, we can regain that light which will illuminate our own path once again and provide the light others may need."[2]

I also love this other scripture Jesus taught to the Nephites about example and light, reiterating again that His light is the way: "Therefore, hold up your light that it may shine unto the world. Behold I am the light which ye shall hold up—that which ye have seen me do" (3 Nephi 18:24).

Trying to be like Him can feel overwhelming since He is God, but we can take comfort in knowing that little acts of kindness—small things we *can* do in our families and communities—make a difference and can inspire others to do the same. We shine like Him when we are patient instead of reacting with frustration when things don't go our way; when we help someone even if it's not convenient; or when we forgive an offense, pass on a warm smile, or give someone a hug and words of encouragement—for "out of small things proceedeth that which is great" (Doctrine and Covenants 64:33).

Self-Reflection:
What small thing could you do for someone else today to be an example of Christ?

69

PRAY ALWAYS

"Jesus stood in the midst, [and] he commanded the multitude that they should kneel down upon the ground. . . . And when he had said these words, he himself also knelt upon the earth; and behold he prayed unto the Father." (3 Nephi 17:13, 15)

THERE ARE SEVERAL PLACES IN 3 NEPHI WHERE CHRIST GIVES INstruction about prayer, providing the pattern and telling them "to watch and pray always, lest ye be tempted" (3 Nephi 18:15). He says to "always pray unto the Father in my name; And whatsoever ye shall ask the Father in my name, which is right, believing that ye shall receive, behold it shall be given unto you. Pray in your families . . . that your wives and your children may be blessed" (3 Nephi 18:19–21).

He prays for the people there, kneeling with them together. Nephi recorded, "The eye hath never seen, neither hath the ear heard, before, so great and marvelous things as we saw and heard Jesus speak unto the Father; . . . and no one can conceive of the joy which filled our souls at the time we heard him pray for us" (3 Nephi 17:16–17).

He also spent time alone praying to the Father. "And it came to pass that Jesus departed out of the midst of them, and went a little way off from them and bowed himself to the earth" (3 Nephi 19:19). "And now Father, I pray unto thee for them, and also for all those who shall believe on their words, that they may believe in me, that I may be in them as thou, Father, art in me, that we may be one" (3 Nephi 19:23).

In this account, Jesus Christ taught the Nephites how to pray and then did it Himself in their behalf. I love the example He set when "he himself also knelt upon the earth; and behold he prayed unto the Father" (3 Nephi 17:15), which to me shows how important He personally thinks prayer is—for us and for Him.

As a small child, I was taught to pray at my mother's knee, and from my childhood to the present I've had the unquestionable knowledge that God hears my prayers. Prayer is as much a part of my life as breathing, and I know without a doubt that prayer connects us with heaven. Like the Savior taught, watching and praying always literally means just that—counseling with God in everything we do, all the time. I have prayed alone and with family and friends. I have prayed in the car, in the forest, by the water, in the mountains, in the grocery store, at school, on an airplane, in the hospital, at home, at church, in the temple, and in many other places. I know I can pray anywhere anytime and that He hears me. And over and over, He has answered.

I *know* He hears your prayers too.

As we move forward preparing for His Second Coming, prophets have counseled: "When we understand and believe that Heavenly Father hears our every prayer, when we strive to obey and live the commandments, we grow in our power to receive continuing revelation. The Holy Ghost can be our constant companion. A feeling of light will stay with us even as the world around us becomes darker."[1]

> *Self-Reflection:*
> *Have you prayed today?*

70

COVENANTS AS "ONE"

"And this shall ye do in remembrance of my body, which I have shown unto you. And it shall be a testimony unto the Father that ye do always remember me. And if ye do always remember me ye shall have my Spirit to be with you." (3 Nephi 18:7)

WHILE THE SAVIOR TAUGHT THE MULTITUDE OF 2,500 NEPHITES— men, women, and children—He still seemed to make a point of focusing on them individually, one at a time. He invited them to "arise and come forth unto me, that ye may thrust your hands into my side, and also that ye may feel the prints of the nails in my hands and in my feet, that ye may know that I am the God of Israel, and the God of the whole earth. . . . And this they did do, going forth one by one" (3 Nephi 11:14–15).

I imagine how long it must have taken for every person there to touch Him, yet He knew it was important and He took the time required to make it happen. His ministry in New Testament times, in the Book of Mormon, and in our day is focused on individuals. The same day Christ let the multitude of "ones" touch Him, He also blessed all the children there—one by one. This teaches us about who He is. He also taught the Nephites about priesthood ordinances and covenants, including baptism, receiving the Holy Ghost, the healing of the sick, and the sacrament.

Covenants are promises we make with God—between Him and us, the "one." Like no two pieces of broken bread are the same in the sacrament tray, none of *us* are exactly the same, and our covenants with God—like baptism, which we renew weekly when we take the sacrament—are between *us* and Him. When we repent daily and prepare to take the sacrament worthily, we receive the blessing of the covenant promise in the scriptures: "And this shall ye do in remembrance of my body, which I have shown unto you. And it shall be a testimony unto the Father that ye do always remember me. And if ye do always remember me ye shall have my Spirit to be with you" (3 Nephi 18:7).

Consider for a moment what gets you up every day. (And I'm not talking about your alarm.) What is it that *really* keeps you going?

I'll tell you what it is for me. Every single day—especially when the circumstances and challenges of life feel too hard—I keep going because of the relationship I have with my Heavenly Father and his Son, Jesus Christ. They are my number one "why." And the reason I have that kind of relationship with Them is because of my covenants—covenants I made in the waters of baptism, and covenants I have made in the temple that have bound me to them.

The ordinance of baptism, which is the first covenant or promise we make with God, is a choice of obedience. We know from scriptural accounts in the New Testament that Jesus Christ Himself was baptized, and He taught that "except a man be born of water and of the Spirit, he cannot enter into the kingdom of God" (John 3:5). And again, here in the Book of Mormon, He teaches the importance of baptism by saying, "Whoso believeth in me, and is baptized, the same shall be saved; and they are they who shall inherit the kingdom of God" (3 Nephi 11:33).

When we are baptized, the ordinance is performed in the *same* way, using the *same* words, for each of us. It is the same when we receive the Holy Ghost through the power of the priesthood by the laying on of hands, and it is also the same with other covenants we make when we go to the temple—the endowment and the sealing covenant of eternal marriage and families.

So, while we all must go through the receiving of these ordinances in the same way—which places us on the covenant path to return home to our Heavenly Father and receive eternal life—the journey on that covenant path is individual. The relationships we build along the way with our Father and our Savior, and the personal revelation and direction we receive to guide us, are specific and distinct to our own personality, needs, trials, challenges, and circumstances.

Because our Father in Heaven knows us and loves us individually as "one," we can be sure He has a plan for us that may look different from someone else's. This, to me, is why it is so important to know Him and hear Him for ourselves. When we seek God through prayer, scripture study, and regular temple attendance, honoring the covenants we make and desiring to feel His presence and guidance in our lives, He reassures us, "I, the Lord, am bound when ye do what I say" (Doctrine and Covenants 82:10).

Self-Reflection:
What do covenants mean to you?

71

Don't Cast Them Out

"Nevertheless, ye shall not cast him out from among you, but ye shall minister unto him and shall pray for him unto the Father in my name. . . . For ye know not but what they will return and repent, and come unto me with full purpose of heart, and I shall heal them." (3 Nephi 18:30, 32)

These scripture verses show the compassion and love the Savior has for those who sin and turn away from Him and His gospel, and they give us clear instructions regarding how we should treat them. He tells us, "Ye shall not cast [them] out from among you, but ye shall minister unto [them] and shall pray for [them]" (3 Nephi 18:30). These verses inspire such hope and healing! Reading these words lifts my heart for those dear to me who have left the Church or have chosen a different path other than the one Christ outlines. I know the power of the Atonement is real—for each and every one of us—for only God can know and understand an individual's heart and why they may be struggling.

Our responsibility is to minister to them—in love—and pray for them.

There was a boy who grew up without a father and also went without many other blessings in life. His Latter-day Saint peers found it easy to taunt and bully him, and during that process, the boy made some mistakes. He started smoking and drinking, and gospel principles began to mean almost nothing to him. The role he was unkindly cast in began to fit. As time passed, his drinking increased, he barely attended school, and he completely stopped going to church. Then one day he was gone, possibly to join the army, some said.

When he returned home about fifteen or sixteen years later, he had changed and embraced the gospel. He had gotten married and had started a family. He was different, but some of his old friends hadn't changed and were unwilling to let him be freed from his past. This was difficult for this man and his family, and eventually they moved away.[1]

After sharing this story, Elder Holland taught, "When a battered, weary swimmer tries valiantly to get back to shore, after having fought strong winds and rough waves which he should never have challenged in the first place, those of us who might have had better judgment, or perhaps just better luck, ought not to row out to his side, beat him with our oars, and shove his head back underwater. That's not what boats were made for. But some of us do that to each other."[2]

We do not know what wounds others are carrying, or why they are in the "place" they are or making the choices they're making. Our Savior, the perfect example of pure love, tells us Himself to not "cast them out" from being included. His healing grace and power is for everyone. If we knew what was really going on behind another's choices or actions—if we saw the whole picture—our misperceptions about others might crumble. If we had all the information, we might see with new eyes—the way He does.

Clayton M. Christensen shared the story of a stake president's wife who showed inspiring unconditional acceptance:

> On one Sunday Sister Virginia Perry, whose husband . . . was president of the Boston Stake, noticed a woman who had quietly found a space on the back row in the . . . chapel, having arrived a few minutes late for sacrament meeting. She was wearing jeans and a T-shirt and had come on her motorcycle. Sister Perry quickly sensed that the woman felt that she didn't fit in. Everyone else was wearing their Sunday best and was sitting with their families. So Sister Perry left her family alone, went to the back pew, and

asked the visitor if she would mind if she sat beside her. When the woman smiled in the affirmative, Sister Perry put her arm around her. The next Sunday Sister Perry came to church wearing Levi's and a T-shirt.[3]

She didn't just notice the woman walk in and wonder who she was, and she didn't just take the good step of inviting the woman to join her family. Instead, she left her own family, went to where this woman sat, and asked to be with her. When we reach out to others with this kind of love and compassion, we can help them come unto Jesus Christ and find healing in Him.

Self-Reflection:
What situation or person in your life can you get better at seeing with God's eyes instead of your own?

72

THE GOSPEL BRINGS JOY

"How beautiful upon the mountains are the feet of him
that bringeth good tidings unto them, that publisheth
peace; that bringeth good tidings unto them of good, that
publisheth salvation; that saith unto Zion: Thy God reigneth!"
(3 Nephi 20:40)

JESUS CHRIST TAUGHT THE NEPHITES SO MANY MARVELOUS TRUTHS after He appeared. I can only imagine their awe, their hope, and the lifting of their burdens that they must have experienced in His presence. In this chapter, He miraculously provides bread and wine to administer the sacrament to them. "Now, there had been no bread, neither wine, brought by the disciples, neither by the multitude; But he truly gave unto them bread to eat, and also wine to drink. And he said unto them: He that eateth this bread eateth of my body to his soul; and he that drinketh of this wine drinketh of my blood to his soul; and his soul shall never hunger nor thirst, but shall be filled" (3 Nephi 20:6–8). When they had all partaken of the sacrament, "they were filled with the Spirit; and they did cry out with one voice, and gave glory to Jesus" (3 Nephi 20:9).

As I read this chapter, and specifically verse 40, I feel joy. Joy from knowing the Savior and having His gospel in my life. Joy from knowing that through Him I can experience true peace, despite my trials or unsettling circumstances, and knowing that He is the only way to gain eternal salvation and return home to my heavenly parents. Joy from understanding the sacrifice He gave of His very life—for me—because to Him, I am worth it. I am enough. His Atonement makes it possible for me to be forgiven when I sin and make mistakes, and that fills me with hope and deep gratitude. I also experience the joy that comes from being taught by the Spirit as I read the sacred text of the Book of Mormon and other scriptures. I feel the confirmation of truth that through Him, my soul need never hunger or thirst with questions about my purpose or the meaning of life.

This knowledge is beautiful, and I feel so much comfort knowing that "God reigneth!" (3 Nephi 20:40).

President Nelson taught:

> When the focus of our lives is on God's plan of salvation . . . and Jesus Christ and His gospel, we can feel joy regardless of what is happening—or not happening—in our lives. Joy comes from and because of Him. He is the source of all joy. . . .
>
> Just as the Savior offers "peace that passeth all understanding," He also offers an intensity, depth, and breadth of joy that defy human logic or mortal comprehension. For example, it doesn't seem possible to feel joy when your child suffers with an incurable illness or when you lose your job or when your spouse betrays you. Yet that is precisely the joy the Savior offers. His joy is constant, assuring us that our "afflictions shall be but a small moment" and be consecrated to our gain. . . .
>
> Joy is powerful, and focusing on joy brings God's power into our lives.[1]

Self-Reflection:
What can you do to feel more joy despite your difficulties?

73

ISAIAH

"And now, behold, I say unto you, that ye ought to search these things. Yea, a commandment I give unto you that ye search these things diligently; for great are the words of Isaiah."
(3 Nephi 23:1)

JESUS CHRIST TELLS THE NEPHITES TO SEARCH THE WORDS OF THE prophets "diligently," including "the words of Isaiah," for they are "great" (3 Nephi 23:1). Searching diligently means doing so with a steady, earnest, and energetic effort, and it's not necessarily something that comes easily. The words of Isaiah, whose name means "Jehovah saves" or "the Lord is salvation," are well known for not being "easy" to understand. But this Old Testament prophet, who lived about 700 years before Christ was born, was quoted more frequently by the Savior, Peter, John the Beloved, and the Apostle Paul than any other prophet of his time. He is quoted 106 times in the Doctrine and Covenants. And in the Book of Mormon, Jacob, Nephi, Abinadi, and the Savior quote thirty-two percent of his book and paraphrase three percent.[1]

Nephi must have felt to include Isaiah's words for a divine purpose—not just for his day but also for ours—when he wrote, "I know that they shall be of great worth unto them in the last days; for in that day shall they understand them; wherefore, for their good I have written them" (2 Nephi 25:8). He understood when he said, "The words of Isaiah are not plain unto you, nevertheless they are plain unto all those that are filled with the spirit of prophecy. . . . Wherefore I shall prophesy . . . according to the spirit which is in me; . . . for behold, my soul delighteth in plainness unto my people, that they may learn" (2 Nephi 25:4).

The scriptures teach that "the testimony of Jesus is the spirit of prophecy" (Revelation 19:10). Our testimony of Him will help us understand Isaiah's words, and we can learn to understand the words of Isaiah better when we study the words of the prophets in the Book of Mormon who teach them. We can ask in prayer to be blessed through the Spirit to have minds that are clear as we study language and symbolism that may be unfamiliar to us.

Nephi quoted Isaiah to his people so he could "more fully persuade them to believe in the Lord their Redeemer" (1 Nephi 19:23). Isaiah wrote and described "repeatedly of the Lord's healing, calming influence. . . . His spirit heals; it refines; it comforts; it breathes new life in to hopeless hearts. It has the power to transform all that is ugly and vicious and worthless in life to something of supreme and glorious splendor. He has the power to convert the ashes of mortality to the beauties of eternity."[2] Those promises are great!

During a sister's rereading of the Book of Mormon, she decided this time she would record her insights along the way in a spiral-bound notebook. She made notes chapter after chapter, but when she came to 1 Nephi 20, which quoted Isaiah, she initially panicked. She had always found Isaiah scriptures hard to understand, but since she had made a commitment to study that way, she decided to persevere. She wrote:

> My recent study of the Old Testament helped my comprehension, as did my thick dictionary and the maps of the ancient Middle East found in the back of the . . . Bible. Still, sometimes I spent weeks puzzling out only a few passages. I studied some verses so much I had them almost memorized, and I found myself thinking about them as I ran errands and cleaned the house.
>
> One day while I was in the car doing errands, an answer came to me about a point that had puzzled me for some time. I had

wondered about Isaiah's choice of words . . . [and] a scripture suddenly came to mind. . . . Suddenly I felt I understood what Isaiah was saying! . . .

Other insights came to me. Weeks turned into months, and I exchanged my spiral notebook for a computer. . . .

These studies took almost an entire year. Not only did my understanding of spiritual things increase, but my own nature softened and changed for the better. My love for others increased, and my desire to do missionary work intensified. I felt I could be part of what Isaiah prophesied about our day by sharing the gospel with others.[3]

She took studying the words of Isaiah to heart, and her understanding and testimony grew in the process.

In this chapter in 3 Nephi, the Savior explained that the words of Isaiah tell us about "all things concerning [the Lord's] people which are of the house of Israel," as well as "the Gentiles," and that all things Isaiah prophesied would be fulfilled (3 Nephi 23:2–3). Some of Isaiah's writings include the scattering of Israel, their gathering and redemption through Jesus Christ, the Restoration of His gospel, and His Second Coming and Millennial reign.

We know that the gathering of Israel is happening now, and according to our prophet, the Lord is hastening it. He tells us, "When we speak of the gathering, we are simply saying this fundamental truth: every one of our Heavenly Father's children, on both sides of the veil, deserves to hear the message of the restored gospel of Jesus Christ." And he promises, "As you continue to read daily from the Book of Mormon, you will learn the doctrine of the gathering, truths about Jesus Christ, His Atonement, and the fulness of His gospel not found in the Bible. The Book of Mormon is central to the gathering of Israel" (see 3 Nephi 5:23–26).[4]

Self-Reflection:
What have you learned or felt from Isaiah's writings?

74

Take It to the Lord

"Concerning those whom the Lord hath chosen, yea, even three who were caught up into the heavens . . . I knew not whether they were cleansed from mortality to immortality—But behold, since I wrote, I have inquired of the Lord, and he hath made it manifest unto me." (3 Nephi 28:36–37)

Before Jesus left the land of Bountiful to return to His Father, he asked His twelve Nephite disciples "one by one" (3 Nephi 28:1) what they desired of Him. Three of them wanted something different than the others—they wanted to remain on the earth without tasting death until the Savior's Second Coming, after "all things shall be fulfilled according to the will of the Father" (3 Nephi 28:7).

As Mormon wrote about this account "according to the record which hath been given" (3 Nephi 28:18), he had some questions of his own about the Three Nephites. He didn't know "whether they were mortal or immortal, from the day of their transfiguration" (3 Nephi 28:17), or if they were "cleansed from mortality to immortality" (3 Nephi 28:36). He took his questions to the Lord and then wrote, "He hath made it manifest unto me" (3 Nephi 28:37).

The Lord gave Mormon answers and understanding.

Have you ever had questions about Church doctrine, policy, history, or other spiritual matters? Have things ever felt confusing or seemed unclear? Like Mormon, we can take any or all of our questions to the Lord. Elder Vern P. Stanfill taught:

> We live in a world in which we will experience challenges to our faith. . . .
>
> Likewise, we might feel embarrassed, uncomfortable, or confused spiritually when we encounter a challenge to our faith. Generally, the intensity and duration of these feelings will depend upon our reaction to them. If we do nothing, doubt, pride, and eventually apostasy may drive us from the light. . . .
>
> We must remember how much our Heavenly Father and His Son love us. They will neither abandon us, nor will They allow us to be overcome if we seek Their help. . . . We must trust in the Lord in order to develop spiritual strength within ourselves.[1]

While one of our sons was serving a mission, he was faced with questions about controversial issues in Church history that weren't always easy to answer. He also came across those who had let their own doubts about Church history grow until it began to affect their testimony and their faith.

He chose to do something different.

Instead of giving in to the doubts others were rehearsing and being confused by his own questions, he increased his study from reliable true sources and diligently, prayerfully sought help and direction from the Lord. Over time, as he did so, his mind was opened to light-filled answers. His understanding and love increased toward the early Church and the leaders who lived during that time. His searching quest brought him closer to God because he turned *toward* Him for answers instead of turning *away*.

The scriptures teach us, "That which is of God is light; and he that receiveth light, and continueth in God, receiveth more light; and that light growth brighter and brighter until the perfect day" (Doctrine and Covenants 50:24).

As we continue on our earthly journey, things will arise that make us pause, wonder, and even question. Church handbooks may get modified or updated, Church programs and policies may change,

Church leaders get called and released, offenses occur, and varied circumstances arrive as time passes that may surprise us, upset us, or feel unsettling.

"There have been times when members or leaders in the Church have simply made mistakes. There have been things said or done that were not in harmony with our values, principles, or doctrine."[2] If needed, we can take *all* of this to the Lord.

We can also hold fast to what we already know, have felt, and have experienced, and we can keep nourishing our faith.

"When faced with questions or tempted to doubt, we should remember the spiritual blessings and feelings that have penetrated our hearts and lives in the past and place our faith in Heavenly Father and His Son, Jesus Christ. . . . To ignore and discount past spiritual experiences will distance us from God."[2]

Self-Reflection:
Is there something you need to take to the Lord instead of trying to deal with it on your own?

PART XII

THE BOOK OF
FOURTH NEPHI
(ABOUT AD 35–321)

"The greatest power of the Book of Mormon is its impact in bringing us closer to Jesus Christ."

—Elder Legrand R. Curtis Jr.[1]

75

LOVE OF GOD

"The love of God . . . did dwell in the hearts of the people. . . .
And surely there could not be a happier people among all
the people who had been created by the hand of God."
(4 Nephi 1:15–16)

THE BOOK OF 4 NEPHI HAS FOUR AUTHORS AND COVERS ALMOST 300 years in forty-nine verses. The first author was Nephi, son of Nephi, who was one of the twelve disciples chosen by Jesus Christ when He appeared and taught the Nephites in Bountiful. The record was then passed on to his son Amos, then to his son (also named Amos), and then to his other son named Ammaron. Ammaron kept them for a time before "being constrained by the Holy Ghost, [to] hide up the records which were sacred" (4 Nephi 1:48).

After the Savior's ministry, a great uniting came among the Nephites and Lamanites as they were truly converted, all choosing to follow and live the gospel of Jesus Christ. Wholly living the commandments—having "all things in common" without designations of "rich and poor, bond and free" (4 Nephi 1:3)—mightily transformed their society for about two hundred years. Their land was free of contention and pride because "the love of God . . . did dwell in [their] hearts" (4 Nephi 1:15), and they were blessed. Mormon declared,

"Surely there could not be a happier people among all the people who had been created by the hand of God" (4 Nephi 1:16).

The teachings of Jesus Christ can transform people through repentance, covenant-making ordinances, and receiving the gift of the Holy Ghost. Andrew C. Skinner, former dean of religious education at Brigham Young University, put it this way:

> A natural by-product of the constant influence and power of the Holy Ghost prevalent among the citizens of this society [in 4 Nephi] was the desire on the part of all the people to deal justly and fairly with each other. Therefore, the people had all things in common and all acts conformed to the pattern of the Savior's life. In sum, complete conversion to the Lord eliminated contention, produced unselfish self-regulation, and resulted in economic and political equality and freedom.
>
> The total lack of contention in the land . . . must have been due to the complete unity of a civilization in which there were neither Nephites, Lamanites, nor any manner of -ites, but all were one in Christ.[1]

This transformation through Jesus Christ happened then and is in the process of happening now.

"It is the mission of the Church of this last dispensation to develop another people who shall live the gospel in its fulness. This people are to become 'pure in heart,' and they shall flourish and be blessed upon the mountains and upon the high places. They shall be the Lord's people. They shall walk with God because they shall be of one heart and one mind, and they shall dwell in righteousness, and there shall be no poor among them."[2]

Nephi mentions the complete lack of contention four times in this chapter (see verses 2, 13, 15, and 18), so it must have been an important point to make. President Oaks counseled, "We should be striving to regain that condition. As modern revelation declares: 'Zion must increase in beauty, and in holiness' (Doctrine and Covenants 82:14). One of the ways prescribed to achieve that increase is 'every man seeking the interest of his neighbor, and doing all things with an eye single to the glory of God' (Doctrine and Covenants 82:19)."[3]

We can know from this book of scripture that "mighty miracles" (4 Nephi 1:13), and apparently pure happiness, come from obedience.

We also know from this book, and from many other examples throughout the Book of Mormon, that when obedience to God's laws ceases, and pride and selfishness creep back in, wickedness follows and lasting happiness becomes unattainable. After a little more than two hundred years had passed, divisions arose again among the people, and then they were again differentiated by -ites. The Nephites, Jacobites, Josephites, and Zoramites were the true worshippers of Christ, and the Lamanites, Lemuelites, and Ishmaelites "did willfully rebel against the gospel of Christ; and they did teach their children that they should not believe, even as their fathers" (4 Nephi 1:38).

Self-Reflection:
What can you learn from the example of the people in
4 Nephi?

PART XIII

THE BOOK OF MORMON
(ABOUT AD 322–421)

"Life moves all too fast. When you feel weak, discouraged, depressed, or afraid, open the Book of Mormon and read."

—President Boyd K. Packer[1]

76

His Porch Light Is Always On

*"And there were no gifts from the Lord, and the Holy Ghost did
not come upon any, because of their wickedness and unbelief."
(Mormon 1:14)*

IN THE BEGINNING OF THIS BOOK, IN CHAPTER ONE, AMMARON GOES
to Mormon, who is about ten years old, and gives him a message because he perceives him as observant and trustworthy despite his young
age. In their conversation, he tells Mormon that when he's older, "Go
to the land Antum, unto a hill which shall be called Shim; and there
have I deposited unto the Lord all the sacred engravings concerning
this people. And behold, ye shall take the plates of Nephi unto yourself . . . and ye shall engrave on the plates of Nephi all the things that
ye have observed concerning this people" (Mormon 1:3–4).

Just a year later, when Mormon is eleven, he sees war beginning in
the borders of Zarahemla. As battles ensued, the Nephites ended up
winning against the Lamanites, and "peace did remain for the space
of about four years, that there was no bloodshed. But wickedness did
prevail upon the face of the whole land, insomuch that the Lord did
take away his beloved disciples, and the work of miracles and healing
did cease because of the iniquity of the people" (Mormon 1:12–13).

By the time Mormon was fifteen, he was still close to God despite what was going on around him. But he wrote that God wasn't giving the people "gifts" anymore and that the Holy Ghost had withdrawn because of their unbelief and wickedness. He was forbidden to "preach unto them, because of the hardness of their hearts; and the land was cursed" (Mormon 1:17).

To me, these scriptures are a reminder that the good things that come from God are gifts, but we should never take them for granted because they can be taken away if we are not living worthy to have them. Our covenants—or sacred promises we make with Him on the covenant path—are a two-way promise, and we are required to keep our end of the agreement. The Lord Himself tells us, "I, the Lord, am bound when ye do what I say; but when ye do not what I say, ye have no promise" (Doctrine and Covenants 82:10).

A sister shared the following experience.

She was raised in the Church and baptized and confirmed at age eight. The gospel was a way of life for her and the Holy Ghost a familiar presence. When she was excommunicated as an adult, she said:

> I felt an almost tangible feeling leave me. I felt like my thinking process had been disrupted and slowed, and making decisions was confusing and difficult. I was anxious and had a hard time feeling peace.
>
> I never realized how losing my membership would change my life completely. I could no longer wear the temple garment or attend the temple. I could not pay my tithing, serve in any calling, take the sacrament, or bear my testimony or pray in church. I no longer had the gift of the Holy Ghost. Most importantly I was not in a covenant relationship with my Savior through the ordinances of baptism and the temple. I was devastated and frightened.[1]

This sister experienced many difficult things as she strove each day of her journey toward getting rebaptized. Even after, she often felt deep guilt and remorse, which caused her unhappiness and worry. But eventually peace came. She describes her covenant relationship with the Savior as "heart-wrenching and tender" as she learned how precious the Atonement of Jesus Christ is.[2]

It's easy to stumble and fall from doubt and sin, but through the gospel of Jesus Christ, we can always return to Him. Elder Gong taught:

> The world is full of mirage, illusion, sleight of hand. So much seems transitory and superficial. . . . Gratefully, there is a way through. . . .
>
> Along life's path, we may lose faith in God, but He never loses faith in us. As it were, His porch light is always on. He invites us to come or return to the covenants that mark His path. He waits ready to embrace us, even when we are "yet a great way off" (Luke 15:20). . . .
>
> In losing our worldly self through covenant belonging, we find and become our best eternal self—free, alive, real—and define our most important relationships. . . . When we covenant all we are, we can become more than we are. Covenant belonging gives us place, narrative, capacity to become. It produces faith unto life and salvation.
>
> Divine covenants become a source of love for and from God and thereby for and with each other.[3]

Self-Reflection:
Have you thanked God today for His gifts in your life?

77

LOVE THEM

"And it came to pass that I, Mormon, did utterly refuse from this time forth to be a commander and leader of this people, because of their wickedness and abomination. Behold, I had . . . loved them, according to the love of God which was in me, with all my heart; and my soul had been poured out in prayer unto my God all the day long for them." (Mormon 3:11–12)

MORMON WENT THROUGH A LOT WITH HIS PEOPLE.

When he was sixteen, he was put in charge of an army of Nephites. The battles that ensued against the Lamanites were rough and bloody. There was also thieving, robbing, murdering, and witchcraft raging throughout the land. This caused great mourning and lamentation among all. When Mormon saw this, he said, "My heart did begin to rejoice within me, knowing the mercies and the long-suffering of the Lord, therefore supposing that he would be merciful unto them that they would again become a righteous people. But behold this my joy was in vain, for their sorrowing was not unto repentance . . . but it was rather the sorrowing of the damned. . . . And they did not come unto Jesus with broken hearts and contrite spirits, but they did curse God, and wish to die" (Mormon 2:12–14).

His people didn't turn toward God when the wickedness and suffering increased; instead, they turned away. His sorrow for them returned when he saw "that the day of grace was passed with them, both temporally and spiritually; for [he] saw thousands of them hewn down in open rebellion against their God, and heaped as dung upon the face of the land" (Mormon 2:15).

The fighting and the wars continued. At times, there were some victories for the Nephites against the Lamanites as Mormon led them, yet he recorded, "Nevertheless the strength of the Lord was not with us; yea, we were left to ourselves, that the Spirit of the Lord did not abide in us; therefore we had become weak like unto our brethren" (Mormon 2:26). His heart continued to sorrow over their wickedness and abominations. More time passed, more battles occurred, and when the Nephites did beat the Lamanites, "a great number of them . . . began to boast in their own strength, and began to swear before the heavens that they would avenge themselves of the blood of their brethren who had been slain by their enemies" (Mormon 3:8–9).

As they readied themselves for the next battle, Mormon told them he was done being their leader. He loved them "according to the love of God which was in [him]," but he had had enough "because of their wickedness and abomination" (Mormon 3:11–12). "Thrice [he] delivered them out of the hands of their enemies," and they "repented not of their sins" (Mormon 3:13). He had to take a stand for truth, even when it hurt his heart.

We need to have courage to do the same—with love and respect—for those who see and choose differently than we do, remembering Elder Holland's words, that "our compassion and our love—fundamental characteristics and requirements of our Christianity—must never be interpreted as compromising the commandments."[1]

President Oaks taught, "The love of God does not supersede His laws and His commandments, and the effect of God's laws and commandments does not diminish the purpose and effect of His love. . . . God's love is so perfect that He lovingly requires us to obey His commandments because He knows that only through obedience to His laws can we become perfect, as He is. For this reason, God's anger and His wrath are not a contradiction of His love but an evidence of His love."[2]

When applying this in our lives and in relationships with those we love and care about, we can work on keeping divisions in the proper context. "When family members are not united in striving to keep the commandments of God, there will be divisions. We do all that we can to avoid impairing loving relationships, but sometimes it happens after all we can do. In the midst of such stress, we must endure the reality that the straying of our loved ones will detract from our happiness, but it should not detract from our love for one another or our patient efforts to be united in understanding God's love and God's laws."[2]

One woman shared her experience with her brother who caused their parents continuous heartache. He was defiant and deceitful, involved with drugs, and resisted all boundaries and rules of their home. His choices eventually caused law enforcement to get involved, and he was faced head-on with the consequences of his actions. For two years, his parents supported his treatment program, and eventually he recovered from his addiction. The sister observed, "I think my parents were extraordinary. They never wavered in their love for [my brother], though they disagreed with and even hated what he was doing to himself and to their family life. But they were committed enough to their family to support [him] in any way necessary to get him through the tough times and onto more solid ground. They practiced the deeper, more sensitive, and extensive gospel of Christ by loving one who had gone astray."[3]

Self-Reflection:
Who needs your unconditional love, and how can you show it?

78

OPEN THE DOOR

"But behold, I was without hope, for I knew the judgments of the Lord which should come upon them; for they repented not of their iniquities, but did struggle for their lives without calling upon that Being who created them." (Mormon 5:2)

MORMON ENDED UP AGAIN LEADING THE NEPHITE ARMIES, BUT HE was "without hope" because they didn't repent or call upon God, and the wars against the Lamanites continued.

Mormon wrote, "I, Mormon, do not desire to harrow up the souls of men in casting before them such an awful scene of blood and carnage as was laid before mine eyes" (Mormon 5:8), but he also knew this record would be for our day as well. "A knowledge of these things must come unto the remnant of these people, and also unto the Gentiles . . . who have care for the house of Israel, that realize and know from whence their blessings come. . . . Behold, they shall come forth according to the commandment of the Lord when he shall see fit, in his wisdom" (Mormon 5:9–10, 13).

Mormon saw the results of watching those around him "repent not of their iniquities" (Mormon 5:2) and not choose God. And it cost the lives of so many in a horrible, violent way. The cost of unrepentant sin can also be a lack of peace, increased inner turmoil, and unrelenting unrest—a horrible way to live the life in which we are told that "men . . . might have joy" (2 Nephi 2:25).

Regarding following the devil instead of God, Nephi also stated, "Others will he pacify, and lull them away into carnal security, that they will say: All is well in Zion; yea, Zion prospereth, all is well—and this the devil cheateth their souls, and leadeth them away carefully down to hell" (2 Nephi 28:21).

But there is another way that truly brings hope—choosing Jesus Christ as our Way. The Savior is always there to help us through anything if we choose to turn to Him, but He never intrudes or comes without our invitation. In the book of Revelation, we read, "Behold I stand at the door, and knock: if any man hear my voice, and open the door, I will come in to him, and will sup with him, and he with me" (Revelation 3:20).

We must decide to "open the door"—with our agency.

President David O. McKay said that taking action "is the most simple test to give knowledge to an individual of which the human mind can conceive. *Doing a thing, introducing it into your very being,* will convince you of whether it is good or whether it is bad. You may not be able to convince *me* of that which you know, but *you know it,* because *you have lived it.*"[1]

Our Savior cares and is concerned for each and every one of us. "And how great is his joy in the soul that repenteth!" (Doctrine and Covenants 18:13).

"Because of His great love for us, a divine love, He wants us to experience the kind of joy that He, Himself, experiences. He said, 'These things have I spoken unto you, that my joy might remain in you, and that your joy might be full' (John 15:11). He will bless us with a genuine peace—mentally, emotionally, physically, spiritually, economically—'not [a peace] as the world giveth' (John 14:27), but a 'peace . . . which passeth all understanding' (Philippians 4:7)."[2]

A sister shared her thoughts about this through poetry:

> "Behold, I stand at the door and knock . . ."
> Within my faithless heart pride deafened me
> Each time I knelt to pray without this door;
> And choosing worldly paths, I strayed from thee,
> For thy still voice was easy to ignore.

Till deep within recesses of my soul,
I heard the echoes of premortal life,
And felt despair I could not console
For time I squandered, lost in sin and strife.
How can it be that thou would come to one,
That thou consider me a soul of worth?
This wondrous thought transcends comparison
As thou art Lord of heaven and this earth.
Each day thy knock still sounds; what is my choice?
O Lord of love and peace, I hear thy voice.[3]

Self-Reflection:
Have you "opened the door" to the Savior today?

79

GREATER THINGS

"And whoso receiveth this record, and shall not condemn it because of the imperfections which are in it, the same shall know of greater things than these." (Mormon 8:12)

MORMON TALKS TO THE HOUSE OF ISRAEL (INCLUDING US) WITH AN invitation to believe in Jesus Christ, repent, be baptized, accept Him as the Redeemer of the world, and "lay hold upon [His] gospel . . . which shall be set before you, not only in this record but also in the record which shall come unto the Gentiles from the Jews" (Mormon 7:8).

This is talking about the Bible and the Book of Mormon—that if you believe one, you will also believe the other. "For behold, this is written for the intent that ye may believe that; and if ye believe that ye will believe this also; and if ye believe this ye will know concerning your fathers, and also the marvelous works which were wrought by the power of God among them" (Mormon 7:9).

Toward the end of his life, Mormon gathered his people together to the land of Cumorah, hoping to gain an advantage over the Lamanites. He wrote, "Knowing it to be the last struggle of my people, and having been commanded of the Lord that I should not suffer the records which had been handed down by our fathers, which were sacred, to fall into the hands of the Lamanites [because the Lamanites would destroy them], therefore I made this record out of the plates of Nephi, and hid up in the hill of Cumorah all the records which had been entrusted to me by the hand of the Lord, save it were these few plates which I gave unto my son Moroni" (Mormon 6:6).

Sometime after he had buried the plates, a great number of Lamanites "did fall upon [his] people" (Mormon 6:9), and all but twenty-four were killed. He also tells us of the many other Nephite armies led by other commanders who were killed. In total, hundreds of thousands of Nephites died. Mormon's "soul was rent with anguish . . . and [he] cried: O ye fair ones, how could ye have departed from the ways of the Lord! O ye fair ones, how could ye have rejected that Jesus, who stood with open arms to receive you! Behold, if ye had not done this, ye would not have fallen. But behold, ye are fallen, and I mourn your loss" (Mormon 6:16–17).

I can barely imagine the magnitude of such a huge number of lives being lost in violent death during this time in the history of the Book of Mormon. It is staggering to contemplate. How deep Mormon's anguish must have been, and how heavy his heart must have felt as he cried out, "O that ye had repented before this great destruction had come upon you" (Mormon 6:22). However, he also looked to the future, knowing how important his record was for coming generations, "the remnant of this people who [were] spared" (Mormon 7:1).

After Mormon's death, his son Moroni, who "remain[ed] alone to write the sad tale of the destruction of [his] people" (Mormon 8:3), spoke to those who will someday receive the Book of Mormon. He asked them not to criticize or disparage it for not being perfect but says, "The same shall know of greater things than these" (Mormon 8:12). The footnote to "greater things" takes us to 3 Nephi, where it says, "And when they shall have received this, which is expedient that they should have first, to try their faith, and if it shall be that they shall believe these things then shall greater things be made manifest unto them" (3 Nephi 26:9).

To me, I also like to think this can apply to receiving personal revelation. As we study the Book of Mormon and seek to hear the Savior's voice through it, we can interpret "greater things" as that which the Spirit can teach us—individually and precisely—about what we need as we walk the covenant path on our journey home to God. Each time I study the scriptures with the Spirit, being prayerfully focused, different passages speak to me depending on where I'm at emotionally and spiritually and what I'm going through at the time. I love how that happens! This strengthens my faith and understanding that God is aware of me and knows exactly what I need to feel and learn.

In a conference address, Elder Benjamin M. Z. Tai taught:

> The Book of Mormon provides spiritual nutrition, prescribes a plan of action, and connects us with the Holy Spirit. Written for us, it contains the word of God in plainness and tells us of our identity, purpose, and destiny. . . .
>
> As a young man beginning my missionary service, I boarded an airplane headed to Australia. Feeling very alone, anxious, and inadequate but having committed to serve, I desperately needed reassurance that what I believed in was true. I prayed and read my scriptures earnestly, but as the flight progressed, my self-doubt intensified and my physical condition deteriorated. After I had been struggling for several hours, a flight attendant walked down the aisle and stopped next to my seat. He took the Book of Mormon I was reading from my hands. He looked at the cover and said, "That's a great book!" then handed the book back to me and kept walking. I never saw him again.
>
> While his words echoed in my ears, I distinctly heard and felt in my heart, "I am here, and I know where you are. Just do your best, for I will take care of the rest." On that airplane above the Pacific Ocean, I received a personal witness through my study of the Book of Mormon and the promptings of the Holy Spirit that my Savior knew who I was and that the gospel was true.[1]

Self-Reflection:
What "greater things" are you learning as you study the Book of Mormon? Record them in your journal.

PART XIV

THE BOOK OF ETHER
(ABOUT 2200–600 BC)

"The Book of Mormon is the best guide to learn how well we are doing and how to do better.... Your copy of the Book of Mormon may be hidden from your view by cares and attention to all you have accumulated in your journey. I plead with you to drink deeply and often from its pages. It has in it the fulness of the gospel of Jesus Christ, which is the only way home to God."

—President Henry B. Eyring[1]

80

HE ANSWERS

"And thus I will do unto thee because this long time ye have cried unto me." (Ether 1:43)

THE BOOK OF ETHER WAS TAKEN FROM TWENTY-FOUR GOLD PLATES that were found by the people of Limhi during the days of King Mosiah. The plates were abridged by Moroni, as directed by God. Ether, the last Jaredite prophet in the book, kept the record of his people who were led to the promised land centuries before the Nephites arrived there.

In this chapter, Ether's genealogy is listed. Many generations back is a man named Jared, who lived during the time when "the Lord confounded the language of the people, and swore in his wrath that they should be scattered upon all the face of the earth" (Ether 1:33). Jared's brother, "being a large and mighty man, and a man highly favored of the Lord," was asked by Jared to "cry unto the Lord, that he will not confound us that we may understand our words" (Ether 1:34).

The brother of Jared did so, "and the Lord had compassion upon their friends and their families also, that they were not confounded" (Ether 1:37). He also prayed to the Lord for other things they needed, and the Lord had compassion on him and answered. He directed them where to go—"a land which is choice above all the lands of the earth" (Ether 1:42)—and told the brother of Jared that it was "because this long time ye have cried unto me" (Ether 1:43).

Our Father in Heaven loved the brother of Jared, and He loves us. He wants us to trust Him, be faithful, and ask Him for what we need. He in turn blesses us and answers our prayers in His wisdom and in His way.

A brother shared the following experience he had with prayer.

One night, at 1:30 a.m., he was jolted awake by the sound of his pager. He was a member of the fire department in Alberta, Canada, and his help was urgently needed. He hurriedly got dressed and looked out the window. He breathed in sharply; one of the homes in the nearby trailer court was engulfed in flames twenty feet high.

Minutes later, the fire chief at the scene told him to get his breathing equipment on—he was backup for the team inside the burning home. Feeling only half-awake and somewhat disoriented, he saw the leaping flames of fire and felt frightened. He had fought different kinds of fires before, but he had been with the department for less than a year and never had to go inside a burning building.

He believed that serving others was the same as serving God, and his work put this into practice, but as he watched the flames shoot higher, intense fear practically paralyzed him.

The order came: "You're going in."

The occupants had already made it out, but the mobile homes close by were at high risk—the fire had to be contained and extinguished. Scared as he was, he ran toward the inferno, praying.

He prayed for his fellow firefighters working by his side. He prayed for the family watching their home burn. He prayed for his wife and children. He prayed for himself and his partner to safely finished the job they needed to do. They could no longer see their way to the other team—the smoke had grown too thick.

He continued praying, and his mind suddenly filled with Lehi's vision of the tree of life. Calmness replaced his fear. He thought about the iron rod, and he knew that the way to find the other team was to follow the fire hose.

It took fifteen minutes to get the fire under control, and as the smoke cleared, he felt overwhelming gratitude for the Lord's help. It was a life-changing experience. The words of the Book of Mormon took on a deeper meaning, and he learned in a powerful way that when we serve others, Heavenly Father watches over us and blesses them through our efforts.[1]

His prayer changed what could have been a different outcome of the fire. And his prayer changed *him* as he "cried unto" God and He answered.

Self-Reflection:
How has prayer changed you?

81

SMALL BUT POWERFUL

"Behold, O Lord, thou canst do this. We know that thou art able to show forth great power, which looks small unto the understanding of men." (Ether 3:5)

THE JAREDITES ARE PREPARING FOR THEIR JOURNEY TO THE "CHOICE land" (the promised land), where the Lord is directing them to go. They needed to do many things to get ready, including building tight barges that were small and light upon the water, according to the instructions God gave them. During the process, the brother of Jared prayed to the Lord, saying, "O Lord, I have performed the work which thou hast commanded me, and I have made the barges according as thou hast directed me. And behold, O Lord, in them there is no light; whither shall we steer? And also we shall perish, for in them we cannot breathe, save it is the air which is in them; therefore we shall perish" (Ether 2:18–19).

The Lord answered and told the brother of Jared how to get fresh air inside the eight barges so they could breathe, and then He asked the brother of Jared, "What will ye that I should prepare for you that ye may have light?" (Ether 2:25).

The brother of Jared thought on this, then he "did molten out of rock sixteen small stones; and they were white and clear, even as transparent glass; and he did carry them in his hands upon the top of the mount" (Ether 3:1). Then with humility and perfect faith, he asked the Lord, "Touch these stones, O Lord, with thy finger, and prepare them that they may shine forth in darkness; and they shall shine forth unto us in the vessels which we have prepared, that we may have light while we shall cross the sea" (Ether 3:4).

I love the brother of Jared's solution and the trust and confidence he showed in the Lord. He knew, "Thou canst do this. We know that thou art able to show forth great power, which looks small unto the understanding of men" (Ether 3:5).

How often do miracles occur in our own lives that some may call small (to the "understanding of men") when in reality those miracles are a show of the Lord's great power in our lives?

We know of prayers to find a lost item—and then it's found. We know of those who pay their tithing with the last of their money and then somehow are blessed to still cover their rent or buy food. We hear stories of healing among the sick or injured when healing seems impossible, examples when a person or friend shows up exactly when needed, and accounts of people being blessed with a hoped-for outcome or righteous desire that occurs against all odds. When we pay attention to "small miracles," our faith in the Lord grows.

One sister shared the following:

> I am grateful for a teacher who encouraged his students to keep a journal of the whisperings or promptings of the Spirit in their lives. He directed us to note what we felt and what resulted. Little things became evident. One day I was frantically trying to complete some assignments and prepare for a trip. I had just been down to the laundry area of the dorm to move my clothes from the washer to the dryer. Unfortunately, all the dryers were in use, and they all had many minutes to go. I went back upstairs discouraged, knowing by the time those dryers finished, I had to be on the road. I had barely returned to my room when I felt prompted to go back downstairs and check the laundry again.
>
> *Foolishness*, I thought—I had just been there, and I didn't have time [to waste]. But because I was trying to listen, I went. Two of the dryers were empty—and I was able to meet all my commitments. Could the Lord possibly have been concerned about smoothing my

way in such a small but, to me, important matter? I have learned since through many such experiences that the Lord will help us in every aspect of our lives when we are trying to serve Him and do His will.[1]

Self-Reflection:
What small but powerful miracles have you witnessed?

82

GOD IS IN THE RAIN

"And they did sing praises unto the Lord . . . and [they] did thank and praise the Lord all the day long; and when the night came, they did not cease to praise the Lord" (Ether 6:9)

JARED, HIS BROTHER, AND THEIR FAMILIES "PREPARED ALL MANNER of food, that thereby they might subsist upon the water, and also food for their flocks and herds . . . [then] got aboard of their vessels or barges, and set forth into the sea, commending themselves unto the Lord their God" (Ether 6:4). Soon after, their barges were tossed upon the sea and blown about by furious winds, but because they were "tight like unto a dish" (Ether 6:7), the water stayed out.

The account goes on to say that the wind never stopped blowing them, and they spent three hundred and forty-four days driven forth upon the water. "And they did sing praises . . . all the day long; and when the night came, they did not cease to praise the Lord" (Ether 6:9).

I'm pretty sure they didn't have a lot of extra room in their barges with the travelers, food, supplies, and animals. I would think the air was probably stifling at times and didn't smell very good because hygiene and cleanliness were probably limited. They also had to be limited on what they could do and how much they could move around.

And with the wind and the tossing about . . . that had to be extremely challenging physically and mentally. I'm sure this entire experience had to feel hard at times, if not most of the time. Yet their example of being grateful and praising the Lord day and night speaks loudly of who they were and what they knew—that God had a plan for them and He was in charge.

Finally, they arrived at their destination. "And when they had set their feet upon the shores of the promised land they bowed themselves down upon the face of the land, and did humble themselves before the Lord, and did shed tears of joy before the Lord, because of the multitude of his tender mercies over them" (Ether 6:12).

Today we don't have the same trials that the Jaredites faced, but we *do* have trials of our own of varying kinds. Sometimes the situation of those trials feels limiting and confining, especially if the trial goes on and on. Do we still praise God during them, day and night, and believe He is leading us to our own "promised land"? Do we recognize His "tender mercies" only once the trial ends, or do we notice them along the way?

President Uchtdorf taught:

Being grateful in times of distress does *not* mean we are pleased with our circumstances. It *does* mean that through the eyes of faith we look beyond our present-day challenges. . . .

Being grateful in our circumstances is an act of faith in God. It requires that we trust God and hope for things we may not see but which are true. By being grateful, we follow the example of our beloved Savior, who said, "Not my will, but thine be done" (Luke 22:42). . . .

When we are grateful to God in our circumstances, we can experience gentle peace in the midst of tribulation. In grief, we can still lift up our hearts in praise. In pain, we can glory in Christ's Atonement. In the cold of bitter sorrow, we can experience the closeness and warmth of heaven's embrace.[1]

God *is* in the rainbow, but He is *also* in the rain!

Self-Reflection:
What hard thing can you praise God for today?

83

BUILDING A FORTRESS

*"Wherefore, I, Moroni, am commanded to write these things
that evil may be done away, and that the time may come that
Satan may have no power upon the hearts of the children of
men, but that they may be persuaded to do good continually,
that they may come unto the fountain of all righteousness and be
saved." (Ether 8:26)*

LIKE OTHER TIME PERIODS IN THE BOOK OF MORMON, WHEN THE
people are righteous and follow God, they are blessed in numerous
ways, but when they turn away from the things of the Spirit, giving
in to pride and greed, wickedness follows. In this chapter, Moroni
mentions that among the Jaredites, "they formed a secret combination, even as they of old; which combination is most abominable and
wicked above all, in the sight of God" (Ether 8:18).

He tells us he was commanded to write these things, warning the
modern Gentiles that "when ye shall see these things come among
you that ye shall awake to a sense of your awful situation. . . . For it
cometh to pass that whoso buildeth it up seeketh to overthrow the
freedom of all lands, nations, and countries; and it bringeth to pass
the destruction of all people, for it is built up by the devil, who is the
father of all lies" (Ether 8:24–25).

What I draw from this is that we need to stand guard against anything that takes us away from the Spirit and the laws of God, and we need to build a protection—a fortress—that prevents Satan from having power over us. Little decisions we make each day—especially praying, reading our scriptures, repenting, and asking for God's help—will have a big impact on keeping us safe and better able to hear the Lord.

When Trent and I pray and read the Book of Mormon regularly—together and individually—we are stronger, more spiritually in tune, and more able to recognize deception quickly. During a recent lesson we attended in a marriage and family relations class in our ward, another sister there said that the more she reads the Book of Mormon, the nicer her husband becomes. We appreciated her comment. It was another example of how much we change and come closer to God when we make righteous choices—part of building our fortress. This sister's husband didn't change—*she* changed. Because when she was closer to the Spirit, their marriage was better.

Elder Ronald A. Rasband counseled:

Satan knows his days are numbered and that time is growing shorter. . . .

For our safety, we must build a fortress of spirituality and protection for our very souls, a fortress that will not be penetrated by the evil one.

Satan is a subtle snake, sneaking into our minds and hearts when we have let our guard down, faced a disappointment, or lost hope. He entices us with flattery, a promise of ease, comfort, or a temporary high when we are low. He justifies pride, unkindness, dishonesty, discontent, and immorality, and in time we can be "past feeling." The Spirit can leave us. "And thus the devil cheateth their souls, and leadeth them away carefully down to hell" (2 Nephi 28:21). . . .

When we build a fortress of spiritual strength, we can shun the advances of the adversary, turn our backs on him, and feel the peace of the Spirit. We can follow the example of our Lord and Savior, who, when tempted in the wilderness, said, "Get thee behind me,

Satan (Luke 4:8)." We each have to learn by the experiences of life how to do that."[1]

Self-Reflection:
How can you make your fortress stronger?

84

THE WITNESS COMES AFTER

"By faith all things are fulfilled—Wherefore, whoso believeth in God might with surety hope for a better world. . . . Faith is things which are hoped for and not seen; wherefore, dispute not because ye see not, for ye receive no witness until after the trial of your faith." (Ether 12:3–4, 6)

IN CHAPTER 12, WE FINALLY COME TO THE DAYS OF ETHER AFTER many Jaredite generations and kings have passed, with some having lived wickedly and some having lived righteously. During the times of wickedness, the words of the prophets were ignored and great destruction and death occurred. When righteousness prevailed, the people prospered—until they again turned away from God.

Ether was a prophet whose words were full of the Spirit of the Lord, and "he did cry from the morning, even until the going down of the sun, exhorting the people to believe in God unto repentance lest they should be destroyed, saying unto them that by faith all things are fulfilled" (Ether 12:3). His prophesies were "great and marvelous," but the people didn't believe "because they saw them not" (Ether 12:5).

We know that this is the principle of faith—hoping for things that we don't see. And in this chapter, Moroni added his own words about faith, saying, "Dispute not because ye see not, for ye receive no witness until after the trial of your faith" (Ether 12:6). Moroni then goes on to give us many scriptural examples of faith found in the Book of Mormon. This is a moving and inspiring account.

When I've chosen to have faith in my life—even when answers or peace seem out of reach—God never lets me down. But I have had to learn that my "witness" to hoping for things I can't see doesn't come until I hold on to faith and trust Him. They also don't come exactly when I want them to—I often have to wait until God decides it's time. There are some things I have faith about that haven't happened yet—and many, many years have passed since I asked—but still, I believe that in God's time, all will be made right. This is faith.

Trent's and my faith was tested for more than two years while he searched for full-time, permanent employment. Trent diligently did his part, searching and applying for more than three hundred jobs related to his field of expertise, periodically updating his resume. He networked often with friends, ward members, and business contacts; he had many interviews, several that were progressive; and we offered repeated prayers and fasts, individually and as a couple, for heavenly help.

As months passed, then the year mark and beyond, the adversary seemed to be working almost as diligently in opposition, stirring up feelings of discouragement and rejection within us. At times the battle felt exhausting, but we forged ahead, holding tight to our faith that God was aware of us and had a plan. On the days that seemed extra tough, we remembered that the Lord had never failed us before when we had faced other hard things, and we knew He was with us in this as well, even though we didn't understand why it was taking so long.

We pondered, "What is the lesson God is trying to teach us?"

One day, a moment of truth occurred and full acceptance of the Lord's will took over. During this change, all worry, fear, questioning, and doubts finally left and with it a heavy weight. Peace filled our hearts, and we made a financial decision that showed complete faith that it would all be okay. Just a few weeks later, Trent was offered a permanent full-time position with a service industry company involved in something he is very qualified in and passionate about. The trial of our faith finally ended. The blessing came, sweeter than ever, and with it significant personal growth.

"All must pass through a refiner's fire, and the insignificant and unimportant in our lives can melt away like dross and make our faith bright, intact, and strong. There seems to be a full measure of anguish, sorrow, and often heartbreak for everyone, including those who earnestly seek to do right and be faithful. Yet this is part of the purging to become acquainted with God."[1]

In the New Testament, the Apostle Peter tells us we should "think it not strange concerning the fiery trial, which is to try you, as though some strange thing happened to you: but rejoice" (1 Peter 4:12–13).

Our faith will grow as we remember that part of *testing* that faith is facing trials. The lesson will be sweeter if we ask what God is trying to teach us rather than giving in to fear, doubt, or despair.

Self-Reflection:
How do the blessings that come from faith prepare us to return home to Heavenly Father?

85

WEAK BECOMES STRONG

"And if men come unto me I will show unto them their weakness. I give unto men weakness that they may be humble; and my grace is sufficient for all men that humble themselves before me; for if they humble themselves before me, and have faith in me, then will I make weak things become strong unto them." (Ether 12:27)

CONTINUING IN CHAPTER 12, AFTER MORONI ENDS HIS DISCOURSE on faith, he talks with the Lord about his and his father's "weakness in writing" (Ether 12:23) and his fears of being mocked by the Gentiles "because of the awkwardness of [their] hands" (Ether 12:24). He compared their writing to the brother of Jared's and felt lacking. He wrote, "Thou has not made us mighty in writing like unto the brother of Jared, for thou madest him that the things which he wrote were mighty even as thou art, unto the overpowering of man to read them" (Ether 12:24).

Isn't it interesting to see Moroni worrying about his "weakness in writing"? After all, this was the son of Mormon, the last prophet of the Book of Mormon, who was brave and strong in so many ways—the man who protected the plates, sealed them with his powerful testimony of their truthfulness, and hid them up until he was sent in 1823 as a glorious resurrected being to reveal them to Joseph Smith (see Joseph Smith—History 1:30–42, 45). And yet *he* was worried about his weakness.

The Lord responded to him in Ether 12:27, teaching us as well: "I give unto men weakness that they may be humble; and my grace is sufficient for all men that humble themselves before me; for if they humble themselves before me, and have faith in me, then will I make weak things become strong unto them."

One sister shared that she doesn't know anyone who enjoys having a weakness. Recently, she has been coping with a lot of them, hounding herself on the fact that she is still not "there yet." She has more things to learn and even more to unlearn. Oftentimes, it's her fear of failure that keeps her from trying to fix what's troubling her.

It would be so much easier if we never had weaknesses, right?

But isn't that what we are here for?

Even though that's not always what she wants to hear, she knows it's true.

In the midst of her turmoil, she received a priesthood blessing. In it, she was told that the weaknesses that were being shown to her would become strengths, and she would be able to look at each day as a victory as she conquered the tasks ahead.

That is a powerful promise. She is learning that those weaknesses, those struggles that we all have, are absolutely crucial—and the scriptures even say that God gives them to us. Without them, our eternal progression would be hindered. Even though it's difficult and painful, she knows she can be grateful for what she still has to learn—to trust God and remember that asking for help will bring peace, eventual healing, and the blessings of His grace.

She reflects often on the story told by Elder Hugh B. Brown:

I was living up in Canada. I had purchased a farm. It was run-down. I went out one morning and saw a currant bush. It had grown up over six feet (two meters) high. It was going all to wood. There were no blossoms and no currants. I was raised on a fruit farm in Salt Lake before we went to Canada, and I knew what ought to happen to that currant bush. So I got some pruning shears and clipped it back until there was nothing left but stumps. It was just coming daylight, and I thought I saw on top of each of these little stumps what appeared to be a tear, and I thought the currant bush was crying. . . . I looked at it and smiled and said, "What are you crying about?" . . . I thought I heard that currant bush say this:

"How could you do this to me? I was making such wonderful growth. I was almost as big as the shade tree and the fruit tree that are inside the fence, and now you have cut me down. Every plant in the garden will look down on me because I didn't make what I should have made. How could you do this to me? I thought you were the gardener here."

That's what I thought I heard the currant bush say, and I thought it so much that I answered. I said, "Look, little currant bush, I am the gardener here, and I know what I want you to be. I didn't intend you to be a fruit tree or a shade tree. I want you to be a currant bush, and someday, little currant bush, when you are laden with fruit, you are going to say, 'Thank you, Mr. Gardener, for loving me enough to cut me down. Thank you, Mr. Gardener.'"[1]

Like the gardener in this story, God knows exactly what He wants us to become and what we need to go through to get there, even if it hurts—even when our weaknesses discourage us and we feel broken when we are cut down to a stump in the tedious growth process.

Moroni went on to write that the Lord said, "Because thou has seen thy weakness, thou shalt be made strong, even unto the sitting down in the place which I have prepared in the mansions of my Father" (Ether 12:37).

Trusting Him reminds us that "the pain we experience in this life is infinitesimal compared to what the Savior endured for us. But because of His sacrifice, He knows perfectly how to succor us. He understands exactly how we feel. And He knows, better than anyone, that our lowest valleys can lead us up to our highest mountains. That our brokenness can give way to godliness."[2]

> ### *Self-Reflection:*
> *What weakness can the Lord help you turn into a strength?*

86

GRACE TO HAVE CHARITY

"And now I know that this love which thou hast had for the children of men is charity; wherefore, except men shall have charity they cannot inherit that place which thou hast prepared in the mansions of thy Father." (Ether 12:34)

TOWARD THE END OF ETHER 12, MORONI TALKS ABOUT HOW MUCH Jesus Christ "loved the world, even unto the laying down of [His] life . . . that [He] mightest take it again to prepare a place for the children of men" (Ether 12:33). He then describes this love as charity, which is "the pure love of Christ" (Moroni 7:47), and tells us that unless we have charity, we "cannot inherit that place" God has prepared for us (Ether 12:34). A few verses later, Moroni "prayed unto the Lord" (Ether 12:36) that the Lord would give grace in that pursuit of charity.

In the book of Moroni, Moroni revisits the words of his father Mormon, expounding further on charity and writing that if men don't have charity, they are nothing. "Charity suffereth long, and is kind, and envieth not, and is not puffed up, seeketh not her own, is not easily provoked, thinketh no evil, and rejoiceth not in iniquity, but rejoiceth in the truth, beareth all things, believeth all things, endureth all things" (Moroni 7:45).

These scriptures—and similar ones in the New Testament (1 Corinthians 13:1–13), Doctrine and Covenants (Doctrine and Covenants 121:45), and elsewhere in the Book of Mormon (2 Nephi 26:30)—remind me how important having charity is for our eternal salvation. I loved that Moroni prayed for *us*—that God would give *us* grace in our quest to be charitable—because it isn't always easy. We need His help and grace to do it. When we choose the "good part" (Luke 10:42), especially in how we view others, and not spend our energy and focus being "troubled about many things" (Luke 10:41) like the Lord admonished Martha, we can hopefully clarify and focus on what matters most—the spiritual more than the temporal.

Choosing to follow Him each day—and having charity for ourselves and others in our human weaknesses—is the good part. And we can follow Him better by daily doing the things that invite the Spirit, like praying and reading the scriptures.

Mormon's counsel was to "pray unto the Father with all the energy of heart, that ye may be filled with this love, which he hath bestowed upon all who are true followers of his Son, Jesus Christ" (Moroni 7:48).

We also have received much counsel in modern times:

"Charity is having patience with someone who has let us down. It is resisting the impulse to become offended easily. It is accepting weaknesses and shortcomings. It is accepting people as they truly are. It is looking beyond physical appearances to attributes that will not dim through time. It is resisting the impulse to categorize others."[1]

"When we have charity, we are willing to serve and help others when it is inconvenient and with no thought of recognition or reciprocation. We don't wait to be assigned to help, because it becomes our very nature. As we choose to be kind, caring, generous, patient, accepting, forgiving, inclusive, and selfless, we discover we are abounding in charity."[2]

During World War II, a large statue of Jesus Christ was damaged during a bombing. When the statue was later found amidst the debris, the people of the town were sad and dismayed. The statue was cherished as a symbol of their religious faith and reverence for God. Eventually, most of the statue's damage was repaired—except the hands. Their loss was too extensive. While deciding what to do next, some suggested hiring a professional sculptor to make a new pair of hands. Others had a different idea. They suggested to leave the sculpture as it was as a reminder of the war. That is what they chose to do, but with one new addition: in front of the statue of Jesus Christ, a sign was added at the base that read, "You are my hands."

Our Savior's hands are always filled with love and charity.

"As we emulate His perfect example, our hands can become His hands; our eyes, His eyes; our heart, His heart. . . . As disciples of Jesus Christ, our Master, we are called to support and heal rather than condemn."[3]

When I am in a place where I feel and recognize promptings from the Spirit, I have been led to do things for others that I normally wouldn't think of doing. They aren't necessarily comfortable to do either, mainly because of my own fears and insecurities, and they're not always convenient because life is busy. But every time I have listened and followed through, acting on those promptings, I have received a sweet lifting of my own heart through experiencing Christ's pure love. Likewise, when others have reached out to me with a kind word, thought, or simple deed, I have also been reminded of His love.

I remember a recent morning when I was feeling especially lonely and down. Trent was gone fulfilling a church assignment, and I was alone in our home. I was missing Utah, my children, my grandchildren, and so many other familiar things. I did what I often do when I am feeling that way—I knelt down by the side of my bed to tell Heavenly Father about what I was experiencing. (And yes, I also shed a few tears—something that comes easily for me.) Within literally seconds of ending my prayer, I received a text from a sister in my new ward who was thinking about me—right then. Her words lifted my heart and reminded me that God was aware of me, had heard me, and was letting me know through someone else that I was not alone—I was loved. That sister's small act of charity brightened my day.

Self-Reflection:
Who do you know that could use some charity?

PART XV

THE BOOK OF MORONI
(ABOUT AD 400–421)

"The Book of Mormon contains the fulness of the gospel of Jesus Christ and... the Holy Ghost will confirm the truth of it time after time to anyone who, with a sincere heart, seeks knowledge unto the salvation of their soul."

—Elder Ruben V. Alliaud[1]

87

MEETING TOGETHER

*"And [they] did meet together oft, to fast and to pray, and to
speak one with another concerning the welfare of their souls."
(Moroni 6:5)*

THE BOOK OF MORONI, WHICH IS THE LAST BOOK IN THE BOOK OF
Mormon, consists of ten chapters, several of which are less than five
verses long. It starts after Moroni ended his abridgment of the book of
Ether. He says, "I had supposed not to have written more, but I have
not as yet perished" (Moroni 1:1).

The Lamanites had put to death every Nephite who refused to
deny Jesus Christ—except for Moroni. He kept wandering and hiding
for his own safety, refusing to ever "deny the Christ" (Moroni 1:3).
He wrote "a few more things" that he hoped would be of worth to
the Lamanites and to us in "some future day" (Moroni 1:4) because
he knew apostasy was coming and that clarification was important.
His final chapters included information about the power Jesus gave
the Nephite disciples to confer the gift of the Holy Ghost, priesthood
ordaining, administering the sacrament, the baptism and fellowship-
ping of Church members, and how meetings are conducted.

As disciples of Christ, meeting together often "to fast and to pray,
and to speak one with another concerning the welfare of [our] souls"

(Moroni 6:5) helps us to be stronger. We need each other! So many times as I've attended weekly Sunday church meetings, gone to ward and stake activities, and listened to general conference, I've been cheered, uplifted, and renewed to keep pressing forward. I've connected with others facing similar challenges, and I've been strengthened by their faith and example.

For example, I wrote the following in my journal:

> Today I am grateful for the opportunity I have each week to go to church and get my spiritual reservoir filled. I am also grateful for ward and stake members who share their experiences—I am strengthened by them. The adversary loves us to feel we are all alone, that no one has it as bad as us and that no one cares. Those are lies. I prayed before I went to church today that I would feel the Lord's Spirit while I was there, and I did in great abundance. I'm continually in awe of my Heavenly Father and how in tune He is with me and my life. I know if we try to do what is right, follow Him, and ask in prayer for His help, He will give it.

On the other hand, I've also had my feelings hurt and questioned the advice or opinions of others while attending church. When this happens, it has caused me to dig deep—deep into my faith. It's helped me evaluate what is most important to me and why I am really there. I've discovered that my most important reason for attending church is my testimony and commitment to God—*He* is the reason. It's what He asks of me, and because I've made covenants with Him, I go. And when it's a struggle, and I get prideful or judgmental because of how others treat me or what they say, I ask for His help to forgive them and I repent, realizing I have weaknesses of my own.

President Oaks said:

> Attendance and activity in a church help us become better people and better influences on the lives of others. In church we are taught how to apply religious principles. We learn from one another. A persuasive example is more powerful than a sermon. We are strengthened by associating with others of like minds. . . .
>
> Some say that attending church meetings is not helping them. Some say, "I didn't learn anything today" or "No one was friendly to me" or "I was offended." Personal disappointments should never

keep us from the doctrine of Christ, who taught us to serve, not to be served. . . .

Our [church attendance] and application of eternal principles draw us closer to God and magnify our capacity to love.[1]

I want to be closer to God, and I want to have an increase of love for others, and going to church and meeting together helps me in those ways.

Self-Reflection:
How does going to church help you?

88

YE MAY KNOW

*"It is given unto you . . . that ye may know good from evil;
and the way to judge is as plain, that ye may know with a
perfect knowledge, as the daylight is from the dark night."*
(Moroni 7:15)

I LOVE THAT GOD GIVES US A WAY TO HAVE DISCERNMENT TO KNOW good from evil. Mormon wrote that it's "plain" to discern, just like the contrast of the light of day from the dark of night (see Moroni 7:15). To me, this feels very comforting. We don't have to be confused if we follow the pattern given to us to figure it out.

"Every thing which inviteth to do good, and to persuade to believe in Christ, is sent forth by the power and the gift of Christ; wherefore ye may know with a perfect knowledge it is of God. But whatsoever thing persuadeth men to do evil, and believe not of Christ, and deny him, and serve not God, then ye may know with a perfect knowledge it is of the devil" (Moroni 7:16–17).

The Light of Christ, or "the light of truth" (Doctrine and Covenants 88:6), is described in the Guide to the Scriptures as "an influence that comes from God and prepares a person to receive the Holy Ghost. It is an influence for good in the lives of all people. One manifestation of the light of Christ is conscience, which helps a person

273

choose between right and wrong."[1] The Book of Mormon tells us it is "given to every man" (Moroni 7:16).

If we "search diligently in the light of Christ, that [we] may know good from evil; and if [we] will lay hold upon every good thing, and condemn it not, [we] certainly will be a child of Christ" (Moroni 7:19).

"How is it possible that ye can lay hold upon every good thing?" (Moroni 7:20). *By faith.*

"You must have faith to pray. You must have faith to ponder the word of God. You must have faith to do those things and go to those places which invite the Spirit of Christ and the Holy Ghost."[2]

Faith helps us lay hold upon the good and not give in to doubt despite the "mocking and pointing" (1 Nephi 8:27) that may come from the "great and spacious building" (1 Nephi 8:26) that represents the "pride of the world" (1 Nephi 11:36).

Elder Gregory A. Schwitzer of the Seventy shares this:

> As I watch the current world moving away from God, I think this building is growing in size. Many find themselves today wandering the halls of the great and spacious building, not realizing that they are actually becoming part of its culture. They often succumb to the temptations and the messages. We eventually find them mocking or chiming in with those who criticize or mock.
>
> For years I thought the mocking crowd was making fun of the way the faithful live their lives, but the voices from the building today have changed their tone and approach. Those who mock often try to drown out the simple message of the gospel by attacking some aspect of the Church's history or offering pointed criticism of a prophet or other leader. They are also attacking the very heart of our doctrine and the laws of God, given since the Creation of the earth. . . .
>
> True disciples of Christ are not looking to make excuses for the doctrine when it doesn't fit the world's current concepts.[3]

We don't need to be confused—we have been taught that the way to judge is "plain" when deciding between good and evil.

Self-Reflection:
Are you confused about anything? How can you find answers?

89

FAITH OVER FEAR

"Perfect love casteth out all fear." (Moroni 8:16)

IN MORONI 8:6 WE READ, "PERFECT LOVE CASTETH OUT ALL FEAR."

The word *fear* brings many thoughts and experiences to my mind. It is something I have felt often in varying degrees in different times throughout my life, and I'm sure most of you have felt it as well. I referenced my first substantial experience with it at the beginning of our first book, *God is With Us*, in regards to losing my father in an aviation accident when I was a young girl. I have also wrestled with its influence many other times, but the more I have experienced it, the more I have come to understand its true source—which isn't God.

Trent has a favorite quote about fear from the movie *After Earth*: "Fear is not real. The only place that fear can exist is in our thoughts of the future. It is a product of our imagination, causing us to fear things that do not at present and may not ever exist. That is near insanity. Do not misunderstand me, danger is very real, but fear is a choice."[1] Even if fear is based in things that aren't real, it definitely *feels* real.

I would think Moroni would have dealt with feeling it too. After all, he witnessed the annihilation of his people, including his own family. He wrote, "I even remain alone to write the sad tale of the destruction of my people. . . . My father hath been slain in battle, and all my kinsfolk, and I have not friends nor whither to go; and how long the Lord will suffer that I may live I know not" (Mormon 8:3, 5).

Elder Rasband taught:

> Fear is not new. The disciples of Jesus Christ, out on the Sea of Galilee, feared the "wind and the waves" in the dark of the night. As His disciples today, we too have our fears. Our single adults fear making commitments such as getting married. Young marrieds . . . can fear bringing children into an increasing wicked world. Missionaries fear lots of things, especially approaching strangers. Widows fear going forward alone. Teenagers fear not being accepted; grade schoolers fear the first day of school; university students fear getting back a test. We fear failure, rejection, disappointment, and the unknown. We fear not being chosen, and on the flip side, we fear being chosen. We fear not being good enough. We fear change, and our fears can escalate to terror.[2]

Elder Stevens told a story about a camping trip he took years ago with his sons and some friends. At one point on the trip, he wanted to do some hiking alone. He let the group know where he was going and then headed off for the afternoon. It was fall, and the scenery was beautiful. After what seemed like a few hours, he decided it was time to return to the campsite before the daylight was gone. Along the way, however, darkness arrived. He had a general idea of where he was, but as the sky grew darker, it became harder to make sure he was still heading toward camp. He said:

> I stopped and tried to logically direct myself, which became more and more difficult in the dark. As my heart started to pound harder and my breathing began to increase, fear began to take over. I found myself walking faster, almost wanting to run, but without knowing which direction to head. Adrenaline coursed through my bloodstream. I realized I needed to take special care so as to not lose rationality or allow panic to overtake my emotions. This, unexpectedly, required considerable concentration.
>
> By now it was dark enough and the temperature cool enough for me to know that our group would be comfortably settled around a campfire, and that if I found the right vantage point, the fire would be visible from a long distance.

It was with great relief that I spotted a golden flicker far off in the distance. Remarkably, this small speck of light provided the perspective necessary to immediately reorient myself and plot my return course. The fear that had been building inside of me dissipated faster than it came and was replaced with peace.[3]

Satan uses whispers of fear in our thoughts to keep us from focusing on God and having faith in Him. He loves to distract us and make us afraid whenever he can and whenever we will listen. If we don't quickly cast him out and recognize where the fears are coming from, it's easy to get caught in a downward spiral of greater emotion, despair, and even darkness. But the scriptures teach us that as we focus on our Savior, choosing to have faith—like the light of the campfire in Elder Stevenson's story—then "cometh the visitation of the Holy Ghost, which Comforter filleth with hope and perfect love" (Moroni 8:26).

When we hold on to faith and the love of our Savior, fear will leave. Fear does not come from Him, "for God hath not given us the spirit of fear; but of power, and of love, and of a sound mind" (2 Timothy 1:7).

"Christ's perfect love gives us the confidence to press through our fears and place our complete trust in the power and goodness of our Heavenly Father and of His Son, Jesus Christ. . . . He loves [us] perfectly. He knows what [our] future holds. He wants [us] to 'be not afraid, only believe' (John 15:10)."[4]

> ### Self-Reflection:
> *What fear are you holding on to that you can give to God?*

90

Come unto Christ

"Yea, come unto Christ, and be perfected in him, and deny yourselves of all ungodliness; and if ye shall deny yourselves of all ungodliness, and love God with all your might, mind and strength, then is his grace sufficient for you, that by his grace ye may be perfect in Christ; and if by the grace of God ye are perfect in Christ, ye can in nowise deny the power of God. And again, if ye by the grace of God are perfect in Christ, and deny not his power, then are ye sanctified in Christ by the grace of God, through the shedding of the blood of Christ, which is in the covenant of the Father unto the remission of your sins, that ye become holy, without spot." (Moroni 10:32–33)

The last chapter in the Book of Mormon begins with an exhortation and promise from Moroni to know if the book is true (see Moroni 10:3–5). This is one of the most shared scriptures from members of The Church of Jesus Christ of Latter-day Saints. Moroni then talks about some gifts of the Spirit in verses 8–18 and eventually gives his conclusion. With his last written words to us, Moroni extends his final invitation—an invitation to "come unto Christ" (Moroni 10:32).

Diony and I also want to finish *our* book with this invitation. We invite you to "come unto Christ."

One of the ways to come unto Christ is to start to understand and use His infinite Atonement. Elder Packer said:

> Jacob described what would happen to our bodies and our spirits except an atonement, an infinite atonement, were made. We should, he said, have become "like unto [the devil]" (see 2 Ne. 9:7–9).
>
> I seldom use the word *absolute*. It seldom fits. I use it now—twice. Because of the Fall, the Atonement was absolutely essential for resurrection to proceed and overcome mortal death.
>
> The Atonement was absolutely essential for men to cleanse themselves from sin and overcome the second death, which is the spiritual death, which is separation from our Father in Heaven. For the scriptures tell us, seven times they tell us, that no unclean thing may enter the presence of God.[1]

What does it really look like in your life "to be perfected in Him" by using His Atonement? We learn in Primary that when we sin, we need to repent—this is using the Atonement. But the Atonement is infinite in how it applies to *all* aspects of our lives and trials on this earth. It also applies in grief, heartache, suffering, trauma, or any other challenges of this mortal life. One way we describe it is pushing into the pain, the hurt, the challenge. As you feel it deeper, express it and then let it go! Give it to Christ and let his Atonement change you. Using the Atonement in this way can be difficult to understand, let alone implement or master, but this has worked for us.

We believe the Atonement is working in your life this very second. That is why Jesus Christ suffered, bled, and died—for you and for us. He suffered for that very trial, challenge, or thought that you're having right now. The Atonement of Jesus Christ is real. It is active. It is now. It is always. We are so grateful for this gift—His very life—and even as writers, we're unable to adequately express our gratitude to Christ for it. I am not sure we can completely comprehend it until we are freed from the bounds of this mortal life.

We urge you to be present! Live in the now! That is where the Holy Ghost dwells. Love your neighbors (all mankind), for this is the way to love God. To love them is to serve them. To serve them, you have to first think about them. So forget yourself, confront fear, and serve others with no thought of what you may get in return, and keep pressing forward on your journey to "come unto Christ, and be perfected in him" (Moroni 10:32).

> ### *Self-Reflection:*
> *Have you come unto Christ? Has your family? Has your neighbor? Has your boss? Listen to hear Him, and follow His guidance to help them come unto Him and hear also.*

CONCLUSION

FROM THE AUTHORS

"Love. Healing. Help. Hope. The power of Christ to counter all troubles in all times—including the end of times. That is the safe harbor God wants for us in personal or public days of despair. That is the message with which the Book of Mormon begins, and that is the message with which it ends."

—Jeffrey R. Holland[1]

91

FOCUS AND TUNE IN

"Again they heard the voice, and they understood it not."
(3 Nephi 11:4)

BEFORE JESUS CHRIST APPEARED TO THE NEPHITES GATHERED TO-gether near the temple in Bountiful, Heavenly Father spoke to them. His voice was "as if it came out of heaven; and [the people] cast their eyes round about, for they understood not the voice which they heard; and it was not a harsh voice, neither was it a loud voice. And it came to pass that again they heard the voice, and they understood it not. And again the third time they did hear the voice" (3 Nephi 11:3–4).

How many times in our own lives do we hear the things going on around us but are not really paying attention?

When Heavenly Father spoke to them the third time, they "did open their ears to hear it; and their eyes were toward the sound there-of; and they did look steadfastly towards heaven, from whence the sound came" (3 Nephi 11:5).

The people of Nephi heard Him when they *focused* on His voice. "And behold, the third time they did understand the voice which they heard" (3 Nephi 11:6). Sixty-four years earlier, in the book of Helaman, a group of Lamanites also heard a voice—God's voice—and it was described as "not a voice of thunder, neither was it a voice of a great tumultuous noise, but behold, it was a still voice of perfect mildness, as if it had been a whisper, and it did pierce even to the very soul" (Helaman 5:30).

God spoke to them then, and He speaks to us today. We hear Him best when we focus and tune in.

Thank you, our dear reader friends, for traveling together with us through the Book of Mormon as we read, pondered, and studied, focusing and tuning in to the ways we and others hear Him! Our prayers for you are that you will find Him there for yourself, for "to be most effective, your experiences with the scriptures must be your own. . . . There is no substitute for the time you spend in the scriptures, hearing the Holy Ghost speak directly to you."[1]

NOTES

Preface

[1] Henry B. Eyring, "Trust in God, Then Go and Do," *Ensign* or *Liahona*, Nov. 2010, 73.

Introduction

[1] Russell M. Nelson, "Hear Him," *Ensign* or *Liahona*, May 2020, 89.

[2] Russell M. Nelson, "Hear Him," 89.

[3] Gordon B. Hinckley, "An Angel from on High, the Long, Long Silence Broke," *Ensign*, Nov. 1979, 8.

[4] Jeffrey R. Holland, "Safety for the Soul," *Ensign* or *Liahona*, Nov. 2009.

Part I: The First Book of Nephi

[1] Russell M. Nelson, "The Book of Mormon: What Would Your Life Be Like Without It?," *Ensign* or *Liahona*, Nov. 2017, 61.

1   Heavenly Parents

[1] *Teachings of Presidents of the Church: Spencer W. Kimball* (2006), 222.

[2] Adapted from Brian K. Taylor, "Am I a Child of God?" *Ensign* or *Liahona*, May 2018, 13.

2   Feeling the Spirit

[1] Russell M. Nelson, "Hear Him," *Ensign* or *Liahona*, May 2020, 90.

[2] Richard G. Scott, "Make the Exercise of Faith Your First Priority," *Ensign* or *Liahona*, Nov. 2014, 93.

[3] Richard G. Scott, "How to Learn by the Spirit" (Brigham Young University Educational Week devotional, Aug. 21, 2007), speeches.byu.edu.

3   Tender Mercies

[1] Gerrit W. Gong, "All Nations, Kindreds, and Tongues," *Ensign* or *Liahona*, Nov. 2020, 38.

4   Blessings of Obedience

[1] Thomas S. Monson, "Dare to Stand Alone," *Ensign* or *Liahona*, Nov. 2011, 62.

[2] Robert D. Hales, "If Ye Love Me Keep My Commandments," *Ensign* or *Liahona*, May 2014, 38.

5   Led by the Spirit

[1] Adapted from Randall K. Bennet, "Your Next Step," *Ensign* or *Liahona*, Nov. 2015, 70.

[2] Dieter F. Uchtdorf, "Our Father, Our Mentor," *Ensign*, June 2016.

6   Escape Quickly

[1] Russell M. Nelson, "The Power of Spiritual Momentum," *Liahona*, May 2022, 99.

7   He Knows All

[1] Thomas S. Monson, "Consider the Blessings," *Ensign* or *Liahona*, Nov. 2012, 89.

8   Lamb of God

[1] Jeffrey R. Holland, "Behold the Lamb of God," *Ensign* or *Liahona*, May 2019, 44.

9   Iron Rod: Word of God

[1] Ezra Taft Benson, "The Power of the Word," *Ensign*, May 1986, 79–80.

[2] Story adapted from Neill F. Marriott, "Abiding in God and Repairing the Breach," *Ensign* or *Liahona*, Nov. 2017, 12.

10   Imperfect Yet "Chosen"

[1] Adapted from Michael Scott Glenn, "In the Book of Mormon there's a story," Facebook, June 14, 2022, https://www.facebook.com/MichaelScottGlenn/posts/pfbid0qKL1QXkmR8KCeS8PD-bVwX5YahtGNdzEUtsda7Etx-muy1SfXYcu1uY6GVtcD8DjGel.

[2] Dieter F. Uchtdorf, "The Love of God," *Ensign* or *Liahona*, Nov. 2009, 22.

[3] Dale G. Renlund, "Latter-day Saints Keep on Trying," *Ensign* or *Liahona*, May 2015, 56.

11   Raw Meat Moments

[1] David B. Haight, "Your Purpose and Responsibility" (Brigham Young University fireside, Sept. 4, 1977), 2–3; speeches.byu.edu.

12   He Will Help Us

[1] Adapted from Ana Saulala, "He Trusts Us with Hard Things, So Trust in Him and Act," *Ensign*, June 2019.

Part II: The Second Book of Nephi

[1] Russell M. Nelson, "The Book of Mormon: What Would Your

Life Be Like Without It?," *Ensign* or *Liahona*, Nov. 2017, 62.

14 "Consecrate Thine Afflictions"

[1] *Merriam-Webster.com Dictionary*, s.v. "consecrate," accessed February 23, 2023, https://www.merriam-webster.com/dictionary/consecrate.

[2] See Ezra Taft Benson, "Beware of Pride," *Ensign*, May 1989.

[3] David A. Bednar, "Meek and Lowly of Heart," *Ensign* or *Liahona*, May 2018, 32.

16 Heavenly GPS

[1] Count Your Blessings," *Hymns*, no. 241.

[2] See Sharon Eubank, "I Pray He'll Use Us," *Liahona*, Nov. 2021, 53–56.

[3] Russell M. Nelson, "Joy and Spiritual Survival," *Ensign* or *Liahona*, Nov. 2016, 82.

17 The Choice

[1] Neal A. Maxwell, "Swallowed Up in the Will of the Father," *Ensign*, Nov. 1995, 24.

[2] Dieter F. Uchtdorf, "Our Heartfelt All," *Liahona*, May 2022, 123.

18 Delight and Ponder

[1] *Teaching of Presidents of the Church: David O. McKay* (2003), 31–32.

19 Trust Him in Weakness

[1] Adapted from Faith Sutherlin Blackhurst, "Being Honest with Myself—and with God," *Liahona*, June 2018.

20 Forgiving Yourself

[1] *Addiction Recovery Program: A Guide to Addiction Recovery and Healing* (2005), Step 8: Seeking Forgiveness.

[2] Boyd K. Packer, "The Brilliant Morning of Forgiveness," *Ensign*, Nov. 1995, 20.

21 I'll Go Where You Want Me to Go

[1] Henry B. Eyring, "He Goes before Us," *Ensign* or *Liahona*, May 2020, 68.

22 We Are the House of Israel

[1] *Come, Follow Me—For Individuals and Families: Old Testament 2022*, 41.

[2] Patrick Kearon, "He Is Risen with Healing in His Wings: We

Can Be More Than Conquerors," *Liahona*, May 2022, 37–38.

23   Deceptions of Satan

[1] James E. Faust, "The Great Imitator," *Ensign*, Nov. 1987, 33–35.

[2] James E. Faust, "The Great Imitator," 33.

24   What Is Good and What Is Evil

[1] Quentin L. Cook, "When Evil Appears Good and Good Appears Evil," *Liahona*, Mar. 2018.

[2] Cardinal News, "Paul Harvey: "If I Were The Devil" (Radio Audio and Transcript, Prophetic Warning for a Nation in 1965)," Mar. 22, 2012, https://www.arlingtoncardinal.com/2012/03/paul-harvey-if-i-were-the-devil-radio-audio-and-transcript/.

Part III: The Book of Jacob

[1] Russell M. Nelson, "The Book of Mormon: What Would Your Life Be Like Without It?," *Ensign* or *Liahona*, Nov. 2017, 62.

26   Spiritually Defining Memories

[1] Gawain and Gayle J. Wells, "Hidden Benefits of Keeping a History," *Ensign*, July 1986.

[2] Neil L. Andersen, "Spiritually Defining Memories," *Ensign* or *Liahona*, May 2020, 21.

27   Firm Minds

[1] Harper Douglas, "Etymology of festus," Online Etymology Dictionary, accessed Feb. 23, 2023, https://www.etymonline.com/word/festus.

[2] D. Todd Christofferson, "Firm and Steadfast in the Faith of Christ," *Ensign* or *Liahona*, Nov. 2018, 32.

[3] Adapted from Kami Crookston, "Raising Our Son in a Partnership with God," *Ensign*, July 2017.

28   The Spirit Speaks Truth

[1] Joseph Fielding Smith, *Doctrines of Salvation*, comp. Bruce R. McConkie (1955), 1:38.

[2] Bruce R. McConkie, *Mormon Doctrine*, 2nd ed. (1966), 359.

[3] Craig C. Christensen, "An Unspeakable Gift from God," *Ensign* or *Liahona*, Nov. 2012, 13.

4 Joseph Fielding Smith, *Doctrines of Salvation*, 1:47–48.

5 Matthew L. Carpenter, "The Blessings of Reading the Book of Mormon Every Day," *Liahona*, Apr. 2022.

29   I Could Not Be Shaken

1 Neil L. Andersen, "Trial of Your Faith," *Liahona*, Nov. 2012, 40.

2 Adam Kotter, "When Doubts and Questions Arise," *Liahona*, Mar. 2015.

3 Dieter F. Uchtdorf, "Come Join With Us," *Ensign* or *Liahona*, Nov. 2013, 23.

Part IV: The Book of Enos

1 Russell M. Nelson, "The Book of Mormon: What Would Your Life Be Like Without It?," *Ensign* or *Liahona*, Nov. 2017, 62–63.

30   Don't Look Backward

1 Dale G. Renlund, "Your Divine Nature and Eternal Destiny," *Liahona*, May 2022, 76.

2 Adapted from Haley S., "Could I Really Live the Law of Chastity?," *Liahona*, Aug. 2020.

Part V: The Book of Jarom

1 Russell M. Nelson, "The Book of Mormon: What Would Your Life Be Like Without It?," *Ensign* or *Liahona*, Nov. 2017, 63.

31   A Pricked Heart

1 *Merriam-Webster.com Dictionary*, s.v. "prick," accessed February 24, 2023, https://www.merriam-webster.com/dictionary/prick.

2 Matthew McBride, "Ezra Thayer: From Skeptic to Believer," in *Revelations in Context* (2016).

Part VI: The Book of Omni

1 Gordon B. Hinckley, "A Testimony Vibrant and True," *Ensign*, Aug. 2005.

32   All Good Things Come from God

1 "How Great Thou Art," *Hymns*, no. 86.

Part VII: The Words of Mormon

1 Boyd K. Packer, "The Book of Mormon: Another Testament of Jesus Christ—Plain and Precious Things," *Ensign* or *Liahona*, May 2005, 8–9.

33   For a Wise Purpose

[1] See Doctrine and Covenants 10, section heading; Doctrine and Covenants 10:14–19, 30–45.

Part VIII: The Book of Mosiah

[1] Tad R. Callister, "The Book of Mormon—a Book from God," *Ensign* or *Liahona*, Nov. 2011, 75.

34   Search Them Diligently

[1] Dean M. Davies, "A Sure Foundation," *Ensign* or *Liahona*, May 2013, 10.

35   Is Not Far Distant

[1] Ulisses Soares, "Take Up Our Cross," *Ensign* or *Liahona*, Nov. 2019, 115.

[2] Russell M. Nelson, "Overcome the World and Find Rest," *Liahona*, Nov. 2022.

36   Willing to Submit

[1] Adapted from Juan A. Uceda, "He Teaches Us to Put Off the Natural Man," *Ensign* or *Liahona*, Nov. 2010, 53–55.

[2] Russell M. Nelson, "Overcome the World and Find Rest," *Liahona*, Nov. 2022.

37   Born of Him

[1] C. Richard Chidester, "How can we be 'born again,' or as King Benjamin phrased it, how can we be 'spiritually begotten' of Christ?," *Ensign*, Apr. 1996.

[2] Jeffrey R. Holland, "Alma, Son of Alma," *Ensign*, Mar. 1977.

38   Seer

[1] Dennis B. Neuenschwander, "Living Prophets, Seers, and Revelators," *Ensign*, Nov. 2000, 40–41.

39   Perception versus Reality

[1] Dale G. Renlund, "Your Divine Nature and Eternal Destiny," *Liahona*, May 2022, 70—75.

40   Blinded

[1] W. Craig Zwick, "Lord, Wilt Thou Cause That My Eyes May Be Opened," *Ensign* or *Liahona*, Nov. 2017, 98.

41   Countenance

[1] *Teachings of the Living Prophets Student Manual* (2010), Chapter 3: Succession in the Presidency.

42   Standing with God

[1] Robert J. Matthews, "Abinadi: Prophet and Martyr," *Ensign*, Apr. 1992.

[2] D. Todd Christofferson, "Our Relationship with God," *Liahona*, May 2022, 80.

[3] Thomas S. Monson, "Dare to Stand Alone," *Ensign* or *Liahona*, Nov. 2011, 67.

43   Where Are We Learning?

[1] Russell M. Nelson, "Hear Him," *Ensign* or *Liahona*, May 2020, 89.

[2] Russell M. Nelson, "Make Time for the Lord," *Liahona*, Nov. 2021, 120.

[3] Russell M. Nelson, "Hear Him," 89.

45   A Chance

[1] *Come, Follow Me—For Individuals and Families: Book of Mormon 2020*, 78.

[2] Russell M. Nelson, "The Power of Spiritual Momentum," *Liahona*, May 2022, 97–98.

Part IX: The Book of Alma

[1] Ezra Taft Benson, "The Book of Mormon Is the Word of God," *Ensign*, May 1975, 63.

46   Stand Fast

[1] Russell M. Nelson, "Labels can be fun," Facebook, July 20, 2022, https://www.facebook.com/russell.m.nelson/posts/623571289129759.

[2] Jean B. Bingham, "Covenants with God Strengthen, Protect, and Prepare us for Eternal Glory," *Liahona*, May 2022, 67.

47   Changed Hearts

[1] Ezra Taft Benson, "Born of God," *Ensign*, Nov. 1989, 6.

[2] Adapted from Gerald A. Mead, "Book of Mormon Principles: A Change of Heart," *Ensign*, June 2004.

48   He Understands

[1] David A. Bednar, "Bear Up Their Burdens with Ease," *Ensign* or *Liahona*, May 2014, 89–90.

49   Hear and Hearken

[1] Gerald N. Lund, "Hear and Hearken," *New Era*, June 1995, 10.

50   In His Strength I Can Do All Things

[1] Evan A. Schmutz, "God Shall Wipe Away All Tears," *Ensign* or *Liahona*, Nov. 2016, 116.

[2] Richard G. Scott, "Agency and Answers: Recognizing Revelation," *Ensign*, June 2014, 50.

52   Nourish the Seed

[1] Richard C. Edgley, "Faith—the Choice is Yours," *Ensign* or *Liahona*, Nov. 2010, 31–32.

[2] Richard C. Edgley, "Faith—the Choice is Yours," 32–33.

[3] Henry B. Eyring, "Gifts of the Spirit for Hard Times," *Ensign*, June 2007, 19.

53   In Thee Is My Joy

[1] Amy A. Wright, "Christ Heals That Which is Broken," *Liahona*, May 2022, 84.

[2] Henry B. Eyring, "Walk in the Light," *Ensign* or *Liahona*, May 2008, 125.

54   Pure Happiness

[1] Joseph F. Smith, quoted in Spencer W. Kimball, "What Is True Repentance?," *New Era*, May 1974, 4.

55   Small and Simple

[1] Adapted from Christoffel Golden Jr., "Small and Simple Things," *Ensign* or *Liahona*, Nov. 2007, 78–80.

[2] David A. Bednar, "By Small and Simple Things Are Great Things Brought to Pass" (Brigham Young University Women's Conference address, Apr. 29, 2011), womensconference.byu.edu.

[3] Dallin H. Oaks, "Small and Simple Things," *Ensign* or *Liahona*, May 2018, 90–92.

56   Give Jesus the Wheel

[1] David Bednar, "Pray Always," *Ensign* or *Liahona*, Nov. 2008, 41–42.

58   Always Prepared

[1] Jeffrey R. Holland, "Tomorrow the Lord Will Do Wonders Among You," *Ensign* or *Liahona*, May 2016, 125.

[2] Russell M. Nelson, "The Power of Spiritual Momentum," *Ensign* or *Liahona*, May 2022, 98.

[3] Russell M. Nelson, "Stand as True Millennials," *Ensign*, Oct. 2016.

[4] Carlos E. Asay, "Opposition to the Work of God," *Ensign*, Nov. 1981, 68.

59   Offense Is a Choice

[1] Marion D. Hanks, "Forgiveness, The Ultimate Form of Love," *Ensign*, Nov. 1973, 21.

Part X: The Book of Helaman

[1] Dallin H. Oaks, "All Men Everywhere," *Ensign* or *Liahona*, May 2006, 80.

60   Pride Causes Weakness

[1] Kevin S. Hamilton, "Then Will I Make Weak Things Become Strong," *Liahona*, May 2022.
[2] Adapted from C. Richard Chidester, "No Place for Pride," *Ensign*, Mar. 1990.
[3] See Ezra T. Benson, "Beware of Pride," *Ensign*, May 1989.

61   Removing Clouds of Darkness

[1] Lynn A. Mickelsen, "Light and Growth," *Ensign*, Sept. 2004.

62   Prophets Testify

[1] Henry B. Eyring, "Finding Safety in Counsel," *Ensign*, May 1997, 25.
[2] N. Eldon Tanner, "Judge Not, That Ye Be Not Judged," *Ensign*, July 1972, 35.

63   Revelation through Pondering

[1] Adapted from Heather J. Johnson, "Finding Answers for Myself," *Ensign*, Feb. 2018.
[2] David A. Bednar, "The Spirit of Revelation," *Ensign* or *Liahona*, May 2019, 90.

64   Mercy, Hope, Love

[1] Adapted from Name withheld, "Feeling God's Love through Repentance," *Liahona* (Digital Only: Young Adults), Dec. 2021.

Part XI: The Book of Third Nephi

[1] Michelle D. Craig, "Spiritual Capacity," *Ensign* or *Liahona*, Nov. 2019, 19.

65   Not in Vain

[1] Russell M. Nelson, "Christ is Risen; Faith in Him Will Move

Mountains," *Liahona*, May 2021, 103–4.

66   The Light of the World

1 Ezra Taft Benson, "The Savior's Visit to America," *Ensign*, May 1987, 4–5.

2 Sharon Eubank, "Christ: The Light That Shines in Darkness," *Ensign* or *Liahona*, May 2019, 73.

3 Russell M. Nelson, "Four Gifts That Christ Offers You" (First Presidency Christmas devotional, Dec. 2, 2018), broadcasts. ChurchofJesusChrist.org.

67   Contention: Not of Him

1 George Q. Cannon, *Millennial Star*, vol. 57, 563.

2 Ezra Taft Benson, "Beware of Pride," *Ensign*, May 1989, 6.

3 Russell M. Nelson, "The Power of Spiritual Momentum," *Liahona*, May 2022, 97–100.

68   The Light of Example

1 Adapted from Carlos Pérez, "The Power of Example," *Liahona*, Feb. 2001.

2 Thomas S. Monson, "Be an Example and a Light," *Ensign* or *Liahona*, Nov. 2015, 88.

69   Pray Always

1 Henry B. Eyring, "Prayers of Faith," *Ensign* or *Liahona*, May 2020, 28.

71   Don't Cast Them Out

1 Adapted from Jeffrey R. Holland, "A Robe, a Ring, and a Fatted Calf" (Brigham Young University devotional, Jan. 31, 1984), speeches.byu.edu.

2 Jeffrey R. Holland, "A Robe, a Ring, and a Fatted Calf."

3 Clayton M. Christensen, *The Power of Everyday Missionaries: The What and How of Sharing the Gospel* (Salt Lake City: Deseret Book, 2013), 139.

72   The Gospel Brings Joy

1 Russell M. Nelson, "Joy and Spiritual Survival," *Ensign* or *Liahona*, Nov. 2016, 82.

73   Isaiah

1 See *Old Testament Student Manual 1 Kings–Malachi*, 3rd ed. (2003), 131.

2 Tad R. Callister, *The Infinite Atonement* (Salt Lake City: Deseret Book, 2000), 206–7.

[3] Julie Cannon Markham, "Immersed in Isaiah," *Ensign*, Mar. 1999.

[4] Russell M. Nelson and Wendy W. Nelson, "Hope of Israel" (worldwide youth devotional, June 3, 2018), supplement to the *New Era* and *Ensign*, 3, ChurchofJesusChrist.org.

74 Take It to the Lord

[1] Vern P. Stanfill, "Choose the Light," *Ensign* or *Liahona*, Nov. 2015, 56–57.

[2] Vern P. Stanfill, "Choose the Light," 57.

Part XII: The Book of Fourth Nephi

[1] LeGrand R. Curtis Jr., "There is Power in the Book," *Ensign* or *Liahona*, Nov. 2019, 70.

75 Love of God

[1] Andrew C. Skinner, "From Zion to Destruction: The Lessons of 4 Nephi," *Ensign*, Sept. 2000.

[2] Marion G. Romney, "Living Welfare Principles," *Ensign*, Nov. 1981, 93.

[3] Dallin H. Oaks, "Brother's Keeper," *Ensign*, Nov. 1986, 23.

Part XIII: The Book of Mormon

[1] Boyd K. Packer, "The Book of Mormon: Another Testament of Jesus Christ—Plain and Precious Things," *Ensign* or *Liahona*, May 2005, 8.

76 His Porch Light Is Always On

[1] Adapted from Name withheld, "Regaining My Covenants," *Ensign*, June 2017.

[2] Name withheld, "Regaining My Covenants."

[3] Gerrit W. Gong, "Covenant Belonging," *Ensign* or *Liahona*, Nov. 2019, 80.

77 Love Them

[1] Jeffrey R. Holland, "Conviction with Compassion," *New Era*, July 2013, 4.

[2] Dallin H. Oaks, "Love and Law," *Ensign* or *Liahona*, Nov. 2009, 26–27.

[3] Adapted from Anonymous, "With Love—from the Prodigal's Sister," *Ensign*, June 1991, 19.

78 Open the Door

[1] David O. McKay, quoted from Ronald T. Halverson, "I Stand at

the Door and Knock," *Ensign* or *Liahona*, Nov. 2004, 32–33.

[2] Ronald T. Halverson, "I Stand at the Door and Knock," 33–34.

[3] Marsha Fowers Paul, "Metamorphosis," *Ensign*, Aug. 1990.

79   Greater Things

[1] Benjamin M. Z. Tai, "The Power of the Book of Mormon in Conversion," *Ensign* or *Liahona*, May 2020, 45–46.

Part XIV: The Book of Ether

[1] Henry B. Eyring, "A Witness," *Ensign* or *Liahona*, Nov. 2011, 68–71.

80   He Answers

[1] Adapted from Tim Schildknecht, "Fighting Fire With Faith," *Ensign*, Jan. 1996.

81   Small But Powerful

[1] Sydney S. Reynolds, "A God of Miracles," *Ensign*, May 2001, 12.

82   God Is in the Rain

[1] Dieter F. Uchtdorf, "Grateful in Any Circumstances," *Ensign* or *Liahona*, May 2014, 76.

83   Building a Fortress

[1] Ronald A. Rasband, "Build a Fortress of Spirituality and Protection," *Ensign* or *Liahona*, May 2019, 108.

84   The Witness Comes After

[1] James E. Faust, "Faith in Every Footstep: the Epic Pioneer Journey," *Ensign*, May 1997, 63.

85   Weak Becomes Strong

[1] Adapted from Hugh B. Brown, "*Liahona* Classic: The Currant Bush," *Liahona*, Mar. 2002.

[2] Maryssa Dennis, "The Beauty of Broken Things," *Ensign* (Digital Only: Young Adults), Aug. 2018.

86   Grace to Have Charity

[1] Thomas S. Monson, "Charity Never Faileth," *Liahona* and *Ensign*, Nov. 2010, 124.

[2] Silvia H. Allred, "Charity Never Faileth," *Ensign* or *Liahona*, Nov. 2011, 115.

[3] Dieter F. Uchtdorf, "Yor Are My Hands," *Ensign* or *Liahona*, May 2010, 68–69.

Part XV: The Book of Moroni

[1] Rubén V. Alliaud, "Found through the Power of the Book of Mormon," *Ensign* or *Liahona*, Nov. 2019, 38.

87 Meeting Together

[1] Dallin H. Oaks, "The Need for a Church," *Liahona*, Nov. 2021, 24–26.

88 Ye May Know

[1] Guide to the Scriptures, "Light, Light of Christ," scriptures.ChurchofJesusChrist.org.
[2] Henry B. Eyring, "Walk in the Light," *Ensign* or *Liahona*, May 2008, 125.
[3] Gregory A. Schwitzer, "Let the Clarion Trumpet Sound," *Ensign*, Nov. 2015, 99–100.

89 Faith over Fear

[1] Will Smith, "Fear is not real," Goodreads, accessed Mar. 1, 2023, https://www.goodreads.com/quotes/1031607-fear-is-not-real-the-only-place-that-fear-can.
[2] Ronald A. Rasband, "Be Not Troubled," *Ensign* or *Liahona*, Nov. 2018, 18.

[3] Gary E. Stevenson, "5 Ways to Conquer Fear," *New Era*, Feb. 2017.
[4] Dieter F. Uchtdorf, "Perfect Love Casteth Out Fear," *Ensign* or *Liahona*, May 2017, 107.

90 Come Unto Christ

[1] Boyd K. Packer, "Atonement, Agency, Accountability," *Ensign*, May 1988, 70.

Conclusion: From the Authors

[1] Jeffrey R. Holland, "Safety for the Soul," *Ensign* or *Liahona*, Nov. 2009, 88.

91 Focus and Tune In

[1] Mark L. Pace, "Conversion is Our Goal," *Liahona*, May 2022, 111.

About the Authors

Diony Heppler (RN, BSN) has been writing books for over fourteen years. Nonfiction is her favorite genre to write, especially if it helps others become closer to Heavenly Father and the Savior Jesus Christ. She grew up in Alaska but has lived in several other states and overseas. She enjoys traveling, hiking, baking, and spending time with family and friends.

Trent has a BS in business management and is passionate about helping others transform and elevate their lives—what his first book is based on. His career has ranged from management in several businesses and industries to running his own consulting and life coaching company. His extroverted nature fuels his love to connect with others. He was born in Canada but has mostly lived in the northwest part of the United States.

Together they are passionate about hearing and following God, serving, writing, and experiencing life side by side. They have ten children and ten grandchildren, and they currently reside in Kansas City, Missouri.

Scan to visit

www.ichoosechrist.com

CEDAR FORT

Publishing & Media

Scan the QR Code
to try our App and get
a 90 day free trial!